COUNTRY
FINISHES
AND EFFECTS

COUNTRY FINISHES
AND EFFECTS

A creative guide to decorating techniques

Judith Miller

First published in the United States
of America in 1997 by
**RIZZOLI INTERNATIONAL
PUBLICATIONS, INC.**
300 Park Avenue South,
New York, NY 10010

First published in the United King-
dom in 1997 by Mitchell Beazley,
an imprint of Reed International
Books Limited, Michelin House,
81 Fulham Road, London SW3 6RB

ISBN 0-8478-2017-3
LC 96-71421

Chief Contributor John Wainwright
Photography James Merrell
Paint demonstrator Mark Done

Editor Julia North
Art Editors Glen Wilkins,
    Emma Boys
Designer Tony Spalding
Production Christina Quigley
Executive Editor Judith More
Art Director Gaye Allen
Executive Art Editor Janis Utton

Produced by Mandarin Offset
Printed in Singapore

Contents

Above and left *In this late 17th-century Swedish house rustic simplicity contrasts with rural sophistication. A well-worn collection of North American painted pine, five-board porch benches and stools (left), and highly elaborate mid-18th-century folk-painted decorations found on the walls and joinery (above).*

Introduction

THE RANGE OF TRADITIONAL DECORATIVE FINISHES AND EFFECTS FOUND IN COUNTRY houses throughout Europe and North America is extensive. Colourwashing and flat-painting, stencilling and folk painting, rustic marbling and folk graining, liming, staining and waxing, adding patina to ceramics and metalwares, are all techniques that can be employed to introduce rustic colours, patterns and textures to numerous surfaces and objects inside and outside a country home. Apart from their aesthetic appeal, the main attraction of most of them is that they are relatively inexpensive and easy to reproduce.

Over the last decade or two there has been a vogue for all things "country". Most noticeable in the highly populated cities and urban areas of Europe, the United States and the countries of Scandinavia, it can perhaps best be expressed as a desire to escape the hectic pace of modern life, and the constantly changing, and often superficial fashions in everyday matters as diverse as food, clothes and the way in which we furnish and decorate where we live. The sought-after alternative is a tranquil, less stressful existence in the country, where food needn't be fast and there's time to smell the roses and fully appreciate and enjoy our homes.

Of course, there is nothing new in this. For example, in both Britain and the United States during the latter part of the 19th century, the Arts and Crafts Movement urged a return to traditional designs and standards of craftsmanship. The period country home, with its robust, hand-crafted furniture and its unpretentious folk art decorations, was celebrated as all that was honest and enduring in the face of the often shoddily mass-produced goods and the fashionable excesses that cluttered many bourgeois urban houses of the period.

Although there is, and there always has been, much that is myth in the country idyll, there is truth in the view that, in terms of interior decoration, country style has been far more consistent and enduring than many of the

Norwegian wood: *part of the painted wooden exterior of the Holmenkollen Park Hotel in Oslo. It was built in 1894 in the "Dragon" (or "Viking") style of architecture, which was part of a romantic revival inspired by Norway's carved-Viking-ship and stave-church traditions. At its heart lies a celebration of cultural roots and an expression of pride in the Viking age.*

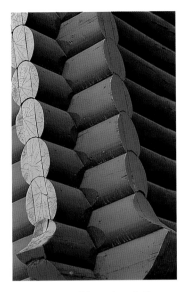

A detail *of the Holmenkollen Park Hotel (opposite). The log walls are painted in traditional Norwegian colours – including cobalt blue.*

This 19th-century Spanish *farmhouse was rebuilt following a serious fire by the architect Jaime Parlade in the 1950s, and converted into a family home. The plastered walls are decorated with a pinkish-terra cotta colourwash tinted with the red-earth coloured pigments that dominate the surrounding countryside.*

External wooden *shutters and yellow colourwashed plastered walls: a combination typical of the rural and coastal regions of southern Europe.*

A traditional English farmhouse *in North Devon. Its cob walls are a mixture of clay subsoil and chopped straw. Lime mortars, plasters and colourwashes were used during their renovation – materials which, unlike modern waterproof equivalents, stop the cob from rotting by allowing evaporation of moisture.*

Durfee House *in St James Park, Los Angeles, California, USA. Built c.1880, in fashionable Eastlake style, its walls are covered with painted wooden shingles. Collectively, such houses are often referred to as "painted ladies". For obvious reasons this one is known as a "pink lady".*

historically important styles of decoration associated with polite city architecture. This is not to say that Baroque, Rococo, Regency and Empire, and other fashions that were largely the preserve of the urban wealthy, were merely a flash-in-the-pan. It is to say, however, that anyone who chooses to decorate or renovate in country style is tapping into a series of decorative conventions that have remained largely unchanged for hundreds, and in some cases, thousands of years.

Limewashing has proved to be the most enduring of all the country paint finishes. Used for thousands of years to decorate and protect plaster, masonry and, to a lesser extent, wood inside and outside the home, it displays a vitality, richness and luminosity of colour that has never been equalled by the vast majority of modern synthetic paints. The chapter on Colourwashing (see pages 17-41) describes where and why it was used, and also shows you how to simulate its appearance by subtly distressing less caustic and easier-to-apply emulsion (latex) paints.

In much the same way that limewash has a unique aesthetic appeal, many of the traditional paints used by the itinerant decorators who plied their trade in the rural communities of Scandinavia, Europe and North America, during the 17th, 18th and 19th centuries, have particular qualities that immediately confer rustic period charm to joinery and furniture around

A dining room *in an early 20th-century Norwegian hunting lodge set in the afforested Hakadal region north of Oslo. The limed pine floorboards, stained log walls and folk-painted wooden beams and ceiling can be found in many other Scandinavian country houses. Note the fantasy marbling in the window recess.*

A detail of *a carved Norwegian cabinet, dated to 1768. The carcass has been painted in a red earth colour, while the middles of the door panels have been fantasy-marbled in typical country style.*

Part of the staircase *in the upper hallway of the hunting lodge shown opposite. The carved wooden balusters, newel post and handrail have all been decorated with a distressed pink-red colourwash.*

Spruce wall panelling *in a mid-18th-century, Norwegian country house. The panels were hand-painted in Italy and are a very high-quality simulation of marquetry work.*

An historically important *interior at Synvis-stua, a mid-17th-century house in the Os region of Norway. Decorated to a tremendously high standard by a Swedish artist in 1744, it incorporates folk-painted walls and ceiling, a folk-grained bed with fantasy marble panels, and a built-in, folk-grained, marbled and folk-painted cupboard.*

the home. Usually mixed on site from locally available pigments and media, they include milk (or casein) paint, primitive oil paints, and egg tempera. Information is also included on how to artificially (and quickly) distress and age them, thereby simulating a process of wear and tear that often takes decades to develop naturally.

From Medieval times to the present day, the walls, floors, furniture and textiles of many country homes have been personalized by their owners with colourful motifs, patterns and pictoral scenes. There have been two basic methods of doing this: stencilling and hand-painting (or "folk art").

Prior to the end of the 19th century most stencils were cut by hand from materials as diverse as oiled card, leather and wood. Taking their inspiration from the surrounding countryside and day-to-day life on the farm, painters and decorators (and many householders themselves) applied rustic motifs such as flowers, leaves, birds, wild and domestic animals to all manner of surfaces. Where stencils were repeated at regular intervals across walls they were in effect being used to emulate patterned wallpapers which, until the last quarter of the 19th century, were very expensive and often only available in urban areas.

To a far greater extent than stencilling, which became increasingly uniform as mass-produced stencil cards were widely disseminated toward the end of the

An English kitchen *displays a range of finishes. Set against bare wooden floorboards and plain-painted walls, the typically eclectic collection of functional and decorative items includes an antique stained and polished Windsor chair, carved wooden spoons and bread and cheese boards, copper, glass and earthenware storage vessels, and a wicker basket.*

A distressed blue *and green painted Mexican cupboard, and a red and blue painted Jamaican stool. Typical examples of simply constructed and brightly coloured folk furniture, they are now in a North American farmhouse.*

In a Spanish kitchen *blue flat-painted and distressed doors introduce a cool colour note. The walls are colour-washed in yellow, which helps to brighten an otherwise small, dark storage area.*

A recreation of a 19th-century *French provincial bathroom, in a Medieval townhouse in the Lot-et-Garonne region of France. The walls have been faux limewashed, using white, yellow ochre and burnt umber pigments. The 19th-century linen press, on the left, has been decorated with a gray-blue, flat-finish, oil-based paint.*

19th century, folk painting allowed the country home-owner (or the artist he employed) to stamp his mark on his environment. At its simplest level, folk art could consist of a few judiciously positioned, simple hand-painted motifs on a cupboard door or along the top of a wall. But in the hands of a talented artist it could stand comparison with some of the mural work in Renaissance Italy.

Examples of sophisticated folk art appear in many countries, but some of the most outstanding are to be found in late-17th, 18th- and 19th-century Swedish and Norwegian houses. Historical events are portrayed with great skill and attention to detail. For the would-be folk artist, reaching this standard is beyond the competence of all but the most gifted.

Far more attainable for the home decorator are the examples of marbling and woodgraining that consistently appear in country homes. The rustic tradition of faux marbling differs in many important respects to its urban counterpart: while much of the latter consists of accurate painted replications of real marbles and other decorative stones, such as porphyry, country versions are often no more than a pastiche of the real thing. In Scandinavia, many country interiors feature riotously coloured and bizarrely veined faux marbled surfaces that are very loosely based on what marble actually looks like, but decoratively are no less impressive for that.

The repeat-pattern stencil frieze *on the plank walls of this cottage near Houston, Texas, USA, was applied by itinerant German painters in the late 19th century. It was uncovered during a recent restoration, when subsequently applied layers of paint were scrubbed away. The early 19th-century, stick-back rocker chair also features a stencilled motif.*

Similarly, country woodgraining ("folk graining") often only crudely suggests the presence of subtly patined and intricately grained and figured real hardwoods – unlike many of the intricately worked simulations in urban houses, where the painted illusion is often indiscernable from real wood, even under close inspection. Again, they are no less impressive for their lack of realism and often their liveliness encourages the onlooker to participate in the joke that lies at the heart of all such painted illusions.

This book also includes a chapter on some of the traditional finishes (liming, staining and wax polishing) that are used to protect and enhance the natural beauty of wood – a material that is at the heart of country style. In addition, there is a chapter on ceramics and metalwares which includes simple techniques for artificially ageing and patining them.

Finally, at the back of the book there are sections describing the tools and materials that you will require (and, in The Directory, where to obtain them), how to prepare surfaces, how to mix paints and glazes and, most important of all, sensible advice on health and safety.

A large Shaker cupboard, *dating from c.1870, with its original red paintwork still intact. While still wet the paint was lightly dragged with a brush in order to simulate the figuring and grain of cherry wood.*

A turn-of-the-18th-century *North American Federal-style interior, with matte-painted pale blue wall panelling, a stencilled floor, and original painted Sheraton fancy chairs flanking a Federal tiger and bird's eye-maple card table.*

Right *A wall-hung cupboard and a chest of drawers, both of utilitarian country construction. Like many of the other wooden storage vessels in the room, they have both been flat-painted – the colours now naturally distressed and showing their age.*

Above and left *Two contrasting uses of limewash. On the North American twig-and-branch table a diluted, untinted wash adds subtle colour and provides protection against moisture and insect infestation. In the wash-room of a French manoir, a more opaque limewash also protects against moisture, and allows the stone walls to breathe.*

Colourwashing

FOR CENTURIES, COLOURWASHING HAS BEEN ONE OF THE MAIN METHODS OF DECORATING the plastered, rendered and wooden surfaces of country houses. There are three basic types of colourwash: limewash, whitewash (distemper), and oil- and water-based paints diluted with water. The latter are usually applied over wood, and allow the underlying figuring and grain to ghost through. Whitewash can be white or coloured, and is mainly used on internal walls. Limewash can also be white or coloured, and is applied to external and internal walls made from traditional country materials, such as wattle and daub, cob, and lime render, which must "breathe" in order to survive.

imewash is one of the oldest of the decorative and protective finishes applied to plaster, masonry and, to a lesser extent, wood. Archeological evidence has revealed that it was employed on primitive buildings around c.8000 BC. It remained in widespread use, particularly in country areas, up to the middle of the 19th century; this followed the introduction of modern building materials and synthetic, mass-produced paints and washes. Thereafter, its use has tended to be restricted to period buildings constructed from traditional materials, such as cob, which would rapidly deteriorate if sealed with modern, non-porous paints. However, in recent years appreciation of its aesthetic properties has also seen a revival in its use on surfaces that don't physically require it. Equally, its appearance can be successfully simulated on internal walls by distressing modern paints and glazes as they dry. (For an illustrated description of the technique of faux lime-washing, see pages 40–1.)

Although the constituents of limewash have been slightly modified at different times and in different places, the basic wash has always been made by first slaking lump lime in water to produce lime putty. The putty itself is then

Left *The plain whitewashed walls serve to throw into relief the painted joinery, stained wooden floorboards and wax-polished furniture in this 18th-century Colonial interior, sympathetically restored by Stephen Mack.*

A keeping room *in an 18th-century house in Rhode Island, USA, that has been lovingly restored by Stephen Mack (a specialist in this field). The plank walls are decorated with milk paint. The lime content of the paint has fungicidal and insecticidal properties which help to preserve the wood – just as limewash protects plastered and rendered surfaces.*

A view of the hearth *in the keeping room restored by Stephen Mack (shown above). While limewash and whitewash were traditionally used on plaster and masonry, such as the lintel and supports of a hearth, the chalky deposits they could leave on clothing if rubbed against made them a less suitable finish than milk paint for wooden panelling, joinery and furniture.*

mixed with water and a water-proofing agent, such as tallow (an animal fat) or raw linseed oil. The result is a milk-like wash which, when brushed over a surface in several coats, dries to an opaque "pure" white. Depending on lighting conditions and the weather, this white can either take on a bright, dazzling luminosity (under strong sunlight), or a darker, matte chalk-like appearance (when it is over-cast or raining).

Much-used alternatives to the basic white limewash are produced by mixing in various pigments. Traditionally, these have ranged from locally available earth colours derived, for example, from different types of clay, to by-products of the mining industry, such as cobalt, copper carbonate, iron- and chrome-oxide, and cadmium. One of the most aesthetically appealing aspects of limewash is that these pigments, when enhanced by the basic limewash mix, display a tremendous purity and vitality of colour. They also subtly mellow as they age, often taking on a rather attractive patchy or streaky appearance as a result of gradual chemical changes in the pigments. Such qualities are usually absent in more uniform, modern mass-produced paints and washes.

Aside from its appearance, it is the various physical properties of limewash that do much to explain its widespread use over the centuries. Primarily, it allows the underlying surface to "breathe". This is particularly important for walls made from materials such as

The kitchen of a timber-frame *period house, which has been recently restored. The modern plaster infills between the wooden stud walls have been decorated with a pale earth-coloured faux limewash, mixed from emulsion (latex) paints. Traditional wattle-and-daub wall infills must be finished with real limewash so that moisture can evaporate from them.*

The walls of this 16th-century *dining room at Frog Pool Farm in Avon, England, have been colourwashed. The pigments used in the mix were ochre and Indian red – colours that provide a harmonious backdrop to the oak-beamed ceiling, and the Cromwellian leather-upholstered dining chairs arranged around a 17th-century oak gateleg table.*

Faux limewash finish *on the walls of another room at Frog Pool Farm, in England (shown right and opposite). There are various methods of distressing a colourwash made from modern synthetic emulsion (latex) paints. One of the most effective is described and illustrated on pages 40–1.*

Distressed, faux limewashed walls *flank a 15th-century wooden door and stone archway at Frog Pool Farm. Now an internal door, it was almost certainly the original front entrance to the farmhouse, which dates back to the reign of Edward III. The Windsor chair is 18th-century; the walnut table is 17th-century.*

Scrubbed faux limewash *walls, above stained oak wall-panelling, in a medieval English priory. The effect can be achieved by dry-brushing a reddish-brown emulsion (latex) paint over a pinky-red eggshell basecoat, or by ragging reddish-brown coloured wax polishes into eggshell basecoat.*

A tinted whitewash *on the plaster walls of a 19th-century farmhouse in East Sussex, England. The colour is produced by powder pigments derived from the local clay. The patchy, streaky look occurred naturally over a period of time as a result of chemical changes in the pigments.*

A kitchen in Devon, England, *has been given a traditional country look by owner Guimond Mounter. Apart from the Windsor chairs, much of the effect is created by the application of a terra cotta-coloured, limewash finish over the walls and the ceiling.*

Traditionally, limewashes were coloured *with earth or mineral pigments available from the surrounding countryside. The terra cotta colour of these limewashed walls, at the other end of the kitchen shown left, is a paler version of the red clay found throughout Devon.*

The kitchen at Huttswell Farm, *a restored period farmhouse in North Devon, England. Modern emulsion (latex) paints could not be used on the traditional cob walls as, unlike the pale green limewash that has been applied, they would trap moisture in the clay subsoil and chopped straw mix and cause it to rot.*

The plaster walls *of one of the bedrooms in the Devon house shown above and opposite were first covered with lining paper, and then decorated with a bright yellow limewash. Exposed to sunlight, limewash has a vitality of colour not often matched by modern synthetic paints.*

The slightly streaky look *of the yellow limewashed walls in another room of the
20th-century house in Devon, England, often occurs naturally with this finish, as a result of
chemical changes that occur in the pigments over time. However, this aesthetically pleasing
effect can also be faked with random brushstrokes during the application of the wash.*

wattle-and-daub and cob (a mixture of clay subsoil and chopped straw), and those covered with lime renders and plasters. It is also essential for walls that have been constructed without a damp-proof course. Because they absorb moisture from the ground or the atmosphere, these traditional building materials would decay if allowed to become permanently damp or saturated with water. Being semi-porous, limewash not only minimizes the absorption of water, but also allows trapped moisture to evaporate without causing it to bubble or blister (as modern paints would do).

In addition to its porosity, limewash also has reasonably powerful disinfectant properties, owing to the fact that slaked lime is caustic. As a result, when applied to timber-frame and half-timbered buildings and to joinery and bare wooden furniture it acts as a deterrent to insect infestation (notably woodworm). For similar reasons, it provides an hygienic, anti-bacterial finish for plastered and rendered kitchen walls. Thus, until the latter part of the 19th century, it was common practice in many farmhouses and country cottages to scrub down the limewashed kitchen walls and repaint them every spring.

Previous page *The upstairs hallway of a hunting lodge, built in 1916 in the Hakadal region of Norway, which lies north of Oslo. The wooden staircase, window frame, and overhead beams have all been decorated with a pinky-orange colourwash.*

The creamy yellow limewash *on these rough-plastered walls (and ceiling) was made by adding yellow ochre pigment to the basic limewash mixture. It is worth noting that when using limewash you should always mix more than enough for the job. If a second batch is required it is rarely the same colour.*

26

A basic white limewash *on the rough-plastered walls of an English country cottage. "Pure" white limewash changes subtly in appearance under different lighting conditions: from a bright and luminous white in strong sunlight to a darker, matte chalky white in overcast conditions.*

In terms of colour, *mixing a traditional limewash is not the exact science that paint manufacturers employ to make modern acrylic emulsion (latex) paints. The exact shade of peach-coloured limewash on these rough-plastered, English-farmhouse walls would have only become apparent once the wash had dried.*

Lime-rendered cob infills *between the exposed wooden studs and beams in a bathroom in an English West-Country cottage. The pale yellow limewash finish is vital as it lets the moisture and condensation of the bathroom evaporate from the substrate of the walls.*

Modern light switches *and power sockets or outlets, which are usually made of white plastic, look incongruous against traditional limewashed walls. Unfortunately, limewash will not stick to plastic so, as here, the switches and sockets have to be painted separately with a colour-matched modern synthetic paint.*

Historically, there has been a long tradition of using limewash on civic, religious and larger domestic buildings in cities and towns. The Romans, for example, applied it to Hadrian's Wall and the famous White Tower at the Tower of London, while in most Scandinavian cities and towns limewash was the most often-used finish on the external walls of both civic and domestic architecture right up until the 1950s. However, it is with vernacular architecture in rural areas, notably farm houses and country cottages, that limewash is most commonly associated.

In the rural houses of Medieval Europe limewash was applied to external and internal walls and the wooden or stone mullions of windows. White and earth colours, such as browns, greens and reds were typical, often providing a base for stencilled geometric or floral patterns, or hand-painted murals. Similarly, plastered walls in many Tudor and Elizabethan houses were limewashed, and augmented with stencils or decorative wall-hangings.

From the 17th century to the middle of the 19th century, throughout Europe, Scandinavia and North America, limewash remained in common use on the rough-plastered internal and external

Left *Pale terra cotta colourwashed walls contrast with the green-painted door and joinery on the landing of a stairwell in an 18th-century French provincial townhouse. The terra cotta pigment is tonally similar to the clay found in the local countryside.*

Plain whitewashed walls *provide a cool, understated backdrop to the simple furnishings of what was once a priest's house near Montalchino in Italy. Together with the wall-hung wooden crucifix, the wrought-iron bed, and the stone floor (relieved only by a threadbare ethnic rug), they contribute to an air of monastic simplicity.*

White colourwashed *bedroom walls in a low-built stone house near Montalchino, Italy. The renovated house was built in 1798.*

An off-white limewash *has been applied to the rough-plastered walls in this bedroom in the Canary Islands. Catching the soft early evening light, it takes on a mellow, restful tone that is in keeping with the furnishings and the purpose of the room.*

A mauve-blue colourwash *on a wood-framed wall panel in a house in the Canary Islands, Spain. Strong colours such as this can be found on plastered walls throughout the Mediterranean. By absorbing sunlight they help to cool otherwise very hot rooms, particularly during the summer months.*

Dark terra cotta-coloured *limewashed walls, in the hallway of a Spanish country house. Although there is a lot of warm red pigment in terra cotta colours, the dark matte surface of this finish provides welcome relief to anyone entering the hall from what can often be very hot daytime heat outside.*

A rough-plastered stone *and terra cotta-tiled sink in the corner of a Spanish country kitchen which, like the walls, have been limewashed. One of the advantages of limewash in this context is its fungicidal properties; another is that it can be easily washed and scrubbed clean and, if necessary, quickly repainted.*

The corner of a salon *in a house on Gran Canary, Spain. The combination of white and terra cotta limewashes makes for a cool, light interior. Although limewash is primarily a rustic finish, it can also show off to good effect sophisticated furnishings, such as the settee, which are more usually found in urban houses.*

Pale lime green *and mauve-blue limewashed walls in a Meditteranean country house.*
They accommodate the need to visually cool the interiors of a house in a hot climate while,
at the same time, not making them too dark or gloomy. Combinations of two (or more)
colours – one more light reflective, one more light absorbent – usually provide the solution.

walls of country houses (although on the internal walls of larger, grander houses it was restricted to less important rooms as wallpaper gradually became available). In Europe, favoured colours, apart from white, varied enormously, although many tended to reflect the local stone or clay – which could range from buff, through mustard, to dusky red. As a general rule, buildings in cooler, northern climes tended to be decorated in more mellow colours such as clotted cream, leaf greens, soft pinks and beige-browns, while in hotter, southern regions brighter, deeper and more vibrant hues, such as acid yellow and mauve-blue, were favoured.

In Scandinavia, limewash (*kalkmålning*) colours ranged from creamy ochre, through tawny orange (with a greenish astringency), to intense salmon pinks and russets. In North America – where the vernacular architecture of pueblo and Spanish New Mexican communities had long been decorated with limewash – 18th-century Colonial-style houses featured smooth- or rough-plastered walls often part-panelled and limewashed in either white or strong, matte earthy colours, such as reddy-browns, marigold, terra cotta, and what could best be described as a dirty buttercup yellow.

One of the drawbacks of using limewash lay in the fact that the process of slaking lime in water to make lime putty produced toxic fumes harmful to the health of the

Above and left *The pink-red colourwashed, wooden plank walls of this 1830s-built Texas house are original. They were discovered when layers of subsequently applied paint were carefully scraped off during a recent restoration of the house. Probably milk paint diluted to a wash with water, the finish allows the underlying figuring of the wood to show through it.*

33

painters and decorators who traditionally mixed it on site. Consequently, from the mid-19th century, limewash was gradually supplanted by whitewash (also known in England as distemper) as a finish for internal walls. Made from whiting, water, animal glue and, if a coloured finish was required, powder pigments, whitewash posed little threat to the health of the decorator and was easier to mix and to apply than limewash.

Nowadays, whitewash (distemper) is available pre-mixed, in white or a range of traditional colours, from specialist suppliers (see The Directory, on pages 170–3). However, you should note that whitewash only keeps for a maximum of three days after it has been mixed, so make sure you prepare the surfaces to be decorated in advance. You should also make sure that the retailer supplies you with a whitewash that contains alum, as this will inhibit mould growth in the wash after it has been applied.

During the second half of the 19th century, the introduction of damp courses, and cement renders and bricks impervious to water meant that walls no longer needed to "breathe" in order to survive. Limewash thus became either unnecessary (or unsuitable) as a finish for walls made from, or incorporating, modern materials. Wallpapers could now be safely used inside, without the fear of them bubbling up or flaking off, while non-porous oil-based paints and, in the 20th century, acrylic (latex) emulsion

Above and right *Two contrasting styles of colourwashing: several applications of a "pure" white limewash on the plank boxing under the stairs produce an opaque finish that hides the figuring and grain of the underlying wood; one coat of a very diluted blue colourwash on a French provincial armoire allows the figuring and grain to show through clearly.*

paints, offered better protection and easier application both inside and outside. However, limewash has remained an essential, authentic and aesthetically desirable finish for buildings constructed of traditional materials.

If you wish to mix and apply a traditional limewash, there are a number of suppliers (see The Directory, on pages 170–3) who can provide you with lime putty, pre-mixed with pigment and raw linseed oil. By purchasing the lime putty pre-mixed you will avoid the hazardous process of slaking lime in water to produce the putty, and thus avoid exposure to toxic fumes. However, you must follow the detailed information on mixing, application and safety supplied by the manufacturer, as the limewash is caustic and can burn if it comes into contact with your skin or, worse, your eyes.

In country areas since the late 17th century a quite distinct method of colourwashing has existed alongside limewashing and, later, whitewashing. Both of the latter decorative techniques are applied in several coats to gradually build up an opaque layer of colour over the underlying surface. The alternative method of colourwashing involves applying very diluted oil- or water-based paints over

Left *An English country dresser used to store and display a collection of riotously colourful glazed pottery. The dresser is made of pine. Its red mahogany-coloured finish is a cross between a loosely brushed colourwash and a crudely dragged folkgrain.*

Pale yellow-cream limewashed *walls brighten this typically crowded English country kitchen. Like the example shown opposite, the pine dresser has been decorated with a finish that suggests both colourwashing and hardwood folkgraining. However, the visibility of large knots on the surface of the dresser clearly identifies the softwood pine underneath.*

Dovetail-jointed blanket boxes *such as this North American example have been made since the 15th century. A variety of woods has been used for their construction. When pine was used it was quite common to decorate it with a wash of colour – often either a diluted milk paint or a translucent glaze of thinned oil paint or varnish.*

Wooden artefacts *regularly exposed to the elements outside are often colourwashed or painted to protect them from damp and, in the worst cases, wet rot. This North American bird house has been limewashed in white and brown. The limewash serves a decorative purpose as well as a functional one.*

a surface to build up subtle veils of semi-translucent colour that allow the underlying surface to "ghost" through them. On walls, the technique requires the application of an opaque basecoat of contrasting colour to the wash or washes on top. Moreover, no effort is usually made to hide any brushmarks in the wash, as they give the finish more texture, pattern and body.

On furniture, the technique is usually different: the thin washes of colour are brushed over bare wood (rather than a painted basecoat), and thus allow the figuring and grain of the wood to partly show through. This method of colourwashing can be achieved using either distemper or milk paint (see pages 42–65) diluted with water, modern emulsion (latex) paints diluted with water, or oil-based paints diluted with white spirit (mineral spirits). The proportions of solvent (water or white spirit) to distemper or paint can vary, depending on how translucent you want the colourwash to be. This is a matter of trial and error, but a good starting point is one part paint to six parts solvent. Test this on an unobtrusive area first and, if it is too opaque, add more solvent until you have achieved the required degree of translucency.

Right *This shelving unit in a North American outhouse holds a range of painted and colourwashed wooden containers. The Shaker-style boxes and the dough and mixing bowls are painted. The coopered pail and the nesting box are colourwashed.*

Faux limewashed walls

The faux limewash shown here is a simulation of limewashing – a traditional finish used on rendered and plastered walls in country areas. You can experiment with different colours (stainers) to change the appearance. As a rule, rust-reds and yellow-browns most closely approximate the earth colours favoured in limewashes. You should note that modern synthetic paints are used in this finish. It must never be applied to traditional cob walls: these need to "breathe", and must only be decorated with real limewash.

WHAT YOU NEED

Masking tape For protecting skirting (base) boards, mantels etc.

White eggshell paint To determine the amount required, measure the walls and refer to the manufacturer's recommended coverage on the container.

Large standard decorator's brush A 10–15cm (4–6in) brush is the most suitable size for applying the basecoat and the faux limewash. However, you can use a paint roller for applying the eggshell basecoat.

Mixing containers Two 2.5 litre (4½ UK pints/ 2½ US quarts) plastic or metal containers.

White matte emulsion (latex) paint You will need about 2.5 litres (4½ UK pints/2½ US quarts) as a base for faux limewash.

Universal stainers Raw umber/burnt sienna.

Acrylic emulsion (latex) glaze About 2.5 litres (4½ UK pints/2½ US quarts). The slow-setting type is best.

Cellulose filler (spackle) About 0.5kg (16oz).

White spirit (mineral spirits) For cleaning eggshell paint from brushes.

Sheets of newspaper Use a type with print that does not bleed too readily when wet.

Lint-free rag Use for wiping off splashes and cleaning brushes.

1 Mask off the surrounding areas. Apply two coats of white eggshell paint, using a large standard decorator's brush or a paint roller. Allow to dry for 24 hours after each coat. Mix 1 litre (1¾ UK pints/ 1 US quart) of limewash glaze as follows: 50 percent white matte emulsion (latex) paint, 10 percent raw umber stainer, 20 percent burnt sienna stainer and 20 percent acrylic emulsion (latex) glaze. Then mix in cellulose filler in a ratio of 15 percent filler to 85 percent glaze. Roughly brush the glaze over a 2sq.m (9sq.ft) wall section, and move quickly to step 2.

2 Take a large single sheet of newspaper and lightly press it over the wet glaze. Peel it off almost immediately and repeat until you have covered all the glaze applied in step 1. The paper will distress the glaze, producing variations in texture and colour across the surface. You should vary the angle at which you apply the paper in order to maximize the irregularity of the finish. Work as quickly as possible, and move on to the next section of wall, repeating steps 1 and 2, as quickly as possible. The distressing should be slightly overlapped on all sections of the wall.

3 When the walls have been completely covered, allow them to dry for at least 8 hours. Then make up about 1 litre (1¾ UK pints/1 US quart) of a second glaze, consisting of 80 percent white matte emulsion (latex) paint and 20 percent acrylic emulsion (latex) glaze. Using a large standard decorator's brush, apply the glaze over the walls. The glaze is slightly translucent and will allow the underlying finish to show through, while, at the same time, toning down the stridency of the pattern. How thickly or thinly you apply this glaze is a matter of choice.

4 The inclusion of cellulose filler (spackle) in the faux limewash glaze has two purposes. First, it introduces a rougher texture to the finish, and in so doing simulates the relatively rough-faced lime render that was traditionally used under limewash. Second, areas of the wall that have a greater build-up of filler on them will absorb more of the second glaze than those areas that have little or no filler. This gives the finish a slightly uneven or patchy appearance, which looks more authentic than if a smooth glaze had been applied in step 1.

Above and left *Useful storage space, provided by a painted yellow pine dresser in typical early New-England style, and a wall-hung pine "keeping box". The latter sits on a simple painted side table; its plank top is made from pine (for economy), its underframe made from a hardwood (for strength and stability).*

Painting & distressing

APART FROM COLOURWASHING, THE MOST COMMON METHOD OF DECORATING WOODEN surfaces inside and outside country homes has been to cover them with paint. However, prior to the end of the 19th century, commercial pre-mixed paints were rarely available outside of the cities and major towns. Consequently, in rural areas itinerant decorators were usually obliged to mix their own paints on site, and augment the limited range of materials that they carried with them with locally available ingredients. Many of these pre-industrial paints have proved to be as practical, colourful and enduring as their modern synthetic equivalents.

efore the start of the 20th century, ready-mixed paints were rarely obtainable outside of large cities and towns. Consequently, the majority of local and itinerant painters and decorators working in the rural areas of North America, Europe and Scandinavia had no option but to mix their own paints on site, drawing, wherever possible, on locally available materials. In order to meet the substantial demand from country dwellers for painted joinery and furniture, they employed a variety of media, many of which had aesthetically pleasing qualities not often matched by most synthetic modern paints.

Limewash (see pages 17–41) had been used to paint wood for thousands of years. However, it did have serious drawbacks as a finish for internal joinery and pieces of furniture, largely due to the fact that if it had been prepared from immature lime putty, or mixed in the wrong proportions, it had a rather unfortunate tendency to leave a chalky deposit on clothing when rubbed against. It was also hazardous and fairly time-consuming to prepare.

Whitewash (also known as distemper, see pages 34–8), had been used to decorate joinery and furniture for hundreds of years, particularly in Norway, Sweden and Denmark. Made from whiting (powdered chalk), water and animal glue, and tinted with powder pigments, it exhibits a pleasing intensity of colour and an attractive soft, powdery, surface bloom as it ages.

During a recent restoration *of an 18th-century American Colonial house by the restorer and interior designer Stephen Mack, five coats of paint (applied at various points during the intervening years) were painstakingly scraped off this wooden wall-panelling to reveal the original bluey-green milk paint.*

Different-coloured paints *have been used to emphasise the architectural features and proportions of this hallway. The stairs, skirting (baseboard) and dado rail have been decorated with blue milk paint, while the dado and field of the wall have been covered with matte green and cream emulsion (latex) paints.*

Fielded-panel cupboard doors *and wall-panelling such as this rarely need to be given additional definition by picking them out in contrasting colours. Indeed, in small rooms, flat-painting them in a single colour helps to "knock them back" so that they do not dominate or reduce the sense of space.*

An early 18th-century *dining room in a house in New Hampshire, USA. The walls are panelled with feather-edge boarding, which has been painted with a green milk paint. The streaking and fading in the paint is caused by prolonged exposure to light and air, and subsequent chemical changes in the pigments.*

The wooden panelled walls *and doors in an Amish farmer's log house have been decorated with green and red milk paint. The colours are matched to those favoured during the 18th century. Built in 1737, the house was moved by its present owners from Lancaster County to Chester County, Pennsylvania, USA.*

However, like limewash, it has durability problems – namely, a tendency to rub off as a result of general wear and tear, and, in damp conditions, to flake and bubble.

Provided the underlying wood was reasonably free from damp, milk paint was a much more durable option. Also known as buttermilk, or casein paint, it offered both the decorator (and the client who was footing the bill) a sensible combination of readily available and inexpensive ingredients, ease of preparation and application, durability, and strength and intensity of colour. Milk paint is made by tinting buttermilk or skimmed milk (which was nearly always available in large quantities in rural farming communities) with earth- or vegetable-coloured pigments (often derived from local clays and plants). A small quantity of lime was usually added to the paint to inhibit any subsequent insect infestation of, or fungal growth on, the underlying wood.

Usually applied directly onto the bare wood in one or two coats, milk paint dries to a smooth finish that has a very subtle sheen. It also presents a clarity and opacity of colour not often matched by modern synthetic paints, and mellows pleasingly with age. An unusual bonus is that during

Left *This bedroom is located under the sloping roof of a converted malt house, built c.1840 on the outskirts of Bath, in England. The tongue-and-grooved wall-panelling and the beams have been decorated with a mid-sheen eggshell oil paint.*

Cream-yellow milk paint *on the plank walls and plaster ceiling, and white emulsion (latex) paint on the panelling around the tub, give this North-American country bathroom a warm, light and airy feel. The ladderback chair and bathside stool have also been painted with white milk paint, now flaking (probably) as a result of the humidity of the room.*

application it gives off a not-unpleasant smell – unlike most modern acrylic emulsion (latex) paints.

Although milk paint was used extensively in Europe and Scandinavia, it is best associated with the 18th- and early 19th-century Colonial interiors along the eastern seaboard of North America. Their plank walls or wall-panelling, mantelpieces, staircases, window frames, skirtings (baseboards), and a wide range of wooden arte-facts were almost invariably coated in this finish.

Anyone wishing to use milk paints on joinery, furni-ture and wooden artefacts today is in a fortunate posi-tion. A number of specialist paint manufacturers (see The Directory, on pages 170–3) produce a wide range of milk paints in authentic Colonial colours – most of which are matched to original 18th- and 19th-century milk-painted joinery and furniture that has survived in historic areas such as Colonial Williams-burg, in Virginia, USA. However, you should note that these modern equivalents do not contain any lime (in conformity with current safety standards).

While milk paints were inexpensive, egg *tempera* was a relatively costly paint, and therefore only requested by

Previous page *A sitting room in a renovated North-American Colonial-style house, dating from the mid-18th century. The plank-panelled walls and the doors have all been decorated with a rust-red milk paint – a colour in harmony with the flagstone floor.*

A typical 19th-century Shaker *interior, with half-height plank walls, doors, windows and joinery all painted with a gray-blue coloured milk paint. The 1840s ladderback chair, which hangs on the wall pegs, is also coated with a traditional oil-based yellow paint. The unusual object standing on the chest of drawers is a beautifully carved and whittled bonnet block.*

In parts of Scandinavia, *notably the rural areas of Sweden and Norway, milk paint was used quite extensively on exterior wooden surfaces. In this example, an external window frame has been picked out with pale blue milk paint to contrast with bare pine wall-cladding.*

White milk-painted *plank walls, brown milk-painted doors and skirtings (baseboards), and a gray-blue milk-painted ladderback chair, in an 1840s plantation farmhouse in Georgia, USA. The chair is 18th-century and originates from the Shenendoah Valley in Virginia.*

The wooden entrance door *and plank walls in the hallway of an Amish log house retain their original Colonial-red milk paint. Specialist paint companies are now reproducing milk paints in the reds, yellows, creams, blues and greens favoured in North America during the Colonial period.*

A view through to the mud room *in a late 18th-century, timber-framed, clapboard house owned and completely restored by Stephen Mack. The wooden plank walls and doors in the foreground have been decorated with an authentic Colonial-period deep red milk paint.*

A view of the keeping room *that lies off the mud room (shown page 51, bottom right), on the ground floor of Stephen Mack's restored 18th-century Colonial-period home. The storage cupboards are milk-painted in a deep Colonial red, as before. Stephen has taken great care to hide or disguise 20th-century conveniences, such as plumbing and electricity.*

A window shutter, *in which the original milk paint has worn away on the fielded panels to reveal the grain of the wood.*

A detail *of a door, dado and skirting (baseboard) in the 18th-century Colonial room shown on page 44. Stephen Mack's rediscovery of the original gray-blue milk paint, albeit somewhat distressed, under layers of more recently painted decorations attests to the durability of this pre-synthetic paint medium.*

wealthier householders, particularly in northern Europe and Scandinavia from the 17th to the 19th century. The expense did not lie so much in the ingredients as in the time it took to dry between coats. In that sense, it was also uneconomic for the itinerant decorator, who maximized his income by completing the work as quickly as possible and by keeping on the move.

Made by mixing powder pigments with linseed oil, water and egg yolk, egg *tempera* is an extremely durable emulsion paint and has a delicate, translucent quality well-suited to better-made pieces of furniture. However, it was rarely used on large expanses of joinery because of the time involved (and therefore the cost). Nowadays, it can be bought pre-mixed in a range of authentic period colours from artists' suppliers (see The Directory, on pages 170–3).

Oil paints were widely used throughout Europe and Scandinavia by the beginning of the 17th century. Like egg *tempera*, they were more expensive than water- and milk-based paints, and thus prior to the 19th century, before many of their ingredients were mass-produced and therefore cheaper, their use tended to be confined to grander country houses.

Right *A modern American house, decorated and furnished to look like a Chester County plank house of the late 18th century. The joinery is painted with an authentic Williamsburg-blue milk paint. The rush-seated ladderback is made of fruitwood.*

Native-American *rugs, pottery and artefacts sit happily alongside painted wooden dressers, cupboards, and a variety of storage vessels – the products of European settlers. The blue milk-painted wooden surfaces are worn and flaking, as a result of years of use and exposure to changing levels of humidity in the air and moisture in the wood.*

A 19th-century *North-American pine wardrobe, subsequently painted with two coats of darker red over paler red milk paint.*

A wall-hung cupboard *recently milk-painted and artificially aged by rubbing down some flat and raised sections with sandpaper.*

An 18th-century cupboard *with its original green milk paint very distressed, but still basically intact. It stands in the kitchen of a farmhouse of the same period in Maine, USA. The wooden storage cupboards under the work surface have been painted (recently) with an off-white milk paint.*

A large, blue milk-painted *cupboard (of Spanish-style construction), naturally distressed and showing its age, in a Santa Fe-style house in New Mexico. Together with the ethnic rugs and the flanking painted chairs, it provides a splash of colour against the white-painted walls and ceiling and the wooden floor and beams.*

However, oil-based paints had certain intrinsic qualities which appealed to decorators and clients alike. First and foremost, they provided an extremely tough and durable finish on wooden joinery and furniture. This gave them an advantage over many water-based emulsions when it came to cleaning and general wear and tear. Second, they gave surfaces a sheen that was both attractive in itself, but also enriched darker colours. Third, although they took much longer to dry than whitewash (distemper) and milk paint, they didn't take as long as egg *tempera*. Fourth, they were quite adaptable, in the sense that when covering large areas they could be applied reasonably thickly, thereby reducing the number of coats required to less than the recommended three. Alternatively, they could be substantially thinned with turpentine (mineral spirits) to make glazes that could be manipulated and softened for specialized decorative techniques such as marbling (see pages 110–13) and wood graining (see pages 126–9).

To mix a traditional oil paint on site was a fairly labour-intensive business. The painter would begin by crushing various pigments into powder form with a muller and ledger (both of which were made of stone). He would then grind the powder into an oil, often adding whiting (ground chalk) to lighten the pigments and give the mixture body. Various types of oil were used, but boiled linseed was the most common.

The next stage was to add turpentine (mineral spirits) and more oil – the proportions varying, depending on which of the three basic coats the painter was mixing. Traditionally, the first coat, or primer, was relatively thin, and for this the oil and turpentine were added half-and-half. The second coat, or undercoat, was thicker, and was thus diluted with two-thirds oil to one-third turpentine. The third, or top, coat was made by diluting with only linseed oil. A traditional alternative to this three-coat system involved mixing a separate and different-coloured primer coat. This can often be seen on early pieces of furniture which retain their original painted finish; the top coat flakes and wears away to reveal the under- and primer coats.

Around the beginning of the 20th century chemists and artists' suppliers began to sell small phials of ground pigments already mixed with oil. Thus, if he could obtain them, the painter only needed to add turpentine (mineral spirits) and more oil to make the paint. While this was undoubtedly labour-saving, there is a school of thought which believes the paints produced from these pre-mixed pigments lack something of the vitality and texture exhibited by the hand-ground versions of earlier centuries.

Regardless of the quality or type of paint used, exposure to the atmosphere, sunlight, humidity and damp, together with day-to-day handling and accidental knocks and bangs, inevitably results in general

A late 18th-century *pine kitchen table. The dark milk paint finish is in a traditional deep red colour, favoured particularly along the eastern seaboard of the United States during the Colonial period. The paint has chipped off and worn away on those areas of the table subject to the greatest wear and tear – namely, the raised edges and corners.*

A late 18th-century *plank-top table and a set of chairs in a North American kitchen. The paint on the chairs is not original and, not surprisingly, shows considerable wear and tear. The yellow milk paint on the table has been reapplied on a number of occasions over the years. Its subtle sheen is a result of regular waxing and polishing.*

An American *storage cupboard. Numerous coats of paint have been applied and partly worn away since it was made in the early 19th century.*

A painted *and artificially distressed pine, wall-hung cupboard in the living area of a recently restored barn in Massachusetts, USA.*

A green-painted *18th-century Welsh press. At some point during the early 20th century it was given a thin coat of whitewash.*

An early 19th-century *American pot cupboard. Made of pine, its single coat of now worn and flaking milk paint is original.*

A naturally distressed *19th-century North-American painted chest of drawers.*
As one might expect, the milk paint has worn away on those parts of the chest subject
to knocks and scuffs during daily use over a long period of time. This effect can be simulated
using the techniques shown and described on pages 62–5.

A painted wooden box *originally intended for storing cutlery, but here requisitioned as a storage box for children's rag dolls. Of simple, butt-jointed construction, such boxes were usually painted (in this case with blue milk paint), or sometimes embellished with simple stencilled or hand-painted motifs.*

A collection *of sycamore, beech, maple and pine cutting boards, some with colourful painted rims. They are all early 20th-century American.*

A painted candle box *embellished with one of the most enduring of country motifs: the heart. This box dates to the early 19th century.*

Shaker-style wooden *storage boxes. Steamed and pinned into shape, they were traditionally painted with milk- or oil-based paints, or varnished.*

A Shaker-style *peg board. The pegs on 18th- and 19th-century boards had distinctive shapes, particular to the community that produced them.*

A painted doll's bench *and a collection of miniature, wood-framed slates, lean against a crudely constructed, painted wooden, open-topped storage box. Although toy-size, the slates would have been used to help children learn to spell, write and read.*

Flaking, cracking and crazing *of the paint on this painted wooden fruit bowl is caused by a combination of factors: accidental knocks, day-to-day handling, and regular exposure to moisture – the latter either eroding the paint from above or lifting it up as it evaporates from the underlying wood.*

A painted cutlery barrel, *the cooper's equivalent of the cabinet-maker's apprentice piece. Prior to the 20th century, the majority of cooking utensils and items of cutlery were carved or turned from wood. Usually they were left as bare wood, or were lightly oiled, but the handles of some pieces were also painted.*

These painted wooden boxes *of various shapes and sizes, are American in origin. Simply constructed, functional objects such as these were invariably made of softwoods, such as pine. Brightly coloured paints provided decoration in the absence of attractive figuring and grain.*

Painted five-board benches *in various sizes. Subject to daily use, the blue milk paint is now worn and chipped, unlike the red oil-based paint on the steamed and pinned round container. Most oil-based paints provide a protective barrier against the intrusion of water and moisture into the underlying wood.*

wear and tear and damage. This can take a variety of forms. For example, exposure to moisture – either on the surface or in the underlying wood – will eventually cause the paint to crack, craze, flake and bubble up. Over a period of time, exposure to direct sunlight will produce chemical changes within the pigments and lead to fading and bleaching. With pieces of furniture, everyday use will wear away the paint on those areas most exposed to contact. On chairs this will be the front rail of the seat and the front legs; on chests of drawers it will be the handles, the leading edges of the drawers, the top and the front feet.

Such naturally occurring damage and wear and tear often has an aesthetic charm that does much to confirm the age of the joinery or piece of furniture in question. Indeed, in terms of desirability and value, distressed painted furniture is often worth more than similar pieces in pristine condition.

It is reasonably easy to reproduce natural wear and tear on modern or recently redecorated pieces of painted furniture using a variety of simple distressing or "antiquing" techniques. These range from applying wax under the paint to cause it to bubble and flake, to spattering with a glaze to simulate woodworm, to cutting back with sandpaper to mimic fading under sunlight and erosion from constant handling. For an illustrated description of these and other techniques, see pages 151–61.

Distressed painted chest

The finish applied to the pine chest of drawers below is designed to simulate the ageing process that naturally occurs on the surface of painted wooden furniture exposed to sunlight, moisture, dirt and general "wear and tear". This finish can be attempted with modern, acrylic (vinyl) water-based paints. However, the most attractive and authentic-looking results are achieved by using the original milk paints favoured by the itinerant decorators of North America, Northern Europe and Scandinavia in the 18th and 19th centuries.

WHAT YOU NEED

White spirit (mineral spirits) Use to remove greasy deposits prior to painting.

Lint-free rag As above.

Sandpaper (medium-grade/grit). For distressing and keying painted surfaces.

Dust sheet (or sheets of old newspaper).

Paints Rust-red and mid-blue milk paint. Plus, if you prefer to mix and colour paints yourself: white casein milk paint powder, and red, black and blue artist's powder pigments.

Plastic bucket (if you mix your own milk paint).

Brushes Three standard decorator's brushes, 5cm (2in), and a small artist's brush.

Furniture wax (clear or tinted).

Electric hot air stripper gun If your gun is not cordless, you will need access to a power outlet and, possibly, an extension cable.

Razor blades Choose a safety-back type.

Clear polyurethane varnish You will need two types: matte and satin (mid-sheen) finish.

Transparent oil (scumble) glaze

Artist's oils Raw umber and black to tint the transparent oil (scumble) glaze.

Wire (steel) wool Grade 00.

Rottenstone A fine, gray limestone powder.

Milk paint can *be bought from specialist suppliers (see pages 170–3) ready mixed, or you can mix your own by tinting white casein milk paint powder with artist's powder pigments (following the maker's instructions).*

1 Remove any dirt or grease from the surface of the chest with a lint-free rag and white spirit (mineral spirits). If the chest has been previously painted or varnished, key the surface by rubbing with medium-grade sandpaper. (On bare wood, apply a coat of primer.) When the surface is clean and dry, apply two coats of rust-red milk paint with a standard decorator's brush. Allow each coat to dry for at least 12 hours.

2 Dissolve a little furniture wax in white spirit (mineral spirits) and, using a standard decorator's brush, apply a thin layer to sections of the chest where you want the blue top coat to bubble up and flake off. For a realistic finish, restrict the wax to those areas where you would expect to find natural "wear and tear", such as the top and bottom of the chest, the handles or pulls and their surrounding areas, and the fronts of drawers.

3 Once the wax has dried apply two coats of mid-blue milk paint, again using a standard decorator's brush and allowing each coat to dry before applying the next. You may find that a third coat of blue is necessary in order to stop the dark red basecoat from "ghosting" through the top coat. However, because you will be distressing the top coat you do not have to be particularly concerned about achieving a perfect finish.

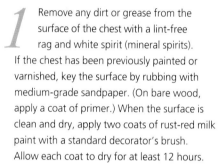

4 When the final blue top coat has thoroughly dried, plug in an electric hot air stripper gun and gently play it about 15cm (6 in) above those areas of the chest where you applied the wax in step 2. As the paint becomes hotter it will start to bubble and blister, detaching itself from the rust-red basecoat below. At this point, you should proceed immediately to step 5, before the paint begins to cool and some of the bubbles start to sink down again.

5 Using a safety-back razor blade, held square-on to the surface of the chest, scrape back and forth across the bubbles. Apply light pressure to flake off small, irregular-shaped patches of the blue top coat and reveal the rust-red basecoat below. On some sections apply more pressure to remove the red basecoat as well, and reveal the bare wood. The amount of paint that you remove is a matter of composition. For the most realistic finish, leave some of the bubbles and restrict exposure of bare wood to those areas where paint tends to be naturally worn away or chipped off, such as the edges of drawers and knobs and around the base. Once you have completed a section move to an adjacent one, repeating steps 4 and 5. If you feel that you have exposed too much bare wood, touch in some of the areas with a small artist's brush and two coats of red milk paint.

6 Using medium-grade (grit) sandpaper, lightly rub back and forth over the distressed areas. The aim is to smooth down the hard edges in the paint around the patches of distressing, and to blend the patches into the surrounding finish. However, by rubbing down with the sandpaper you can also slightly cut back, and therefore lighten, areas of blue to simulate the natural fading that develops on painted wooden furniture as a result of prolonged exposure to sunlight.

7 At this stage, if you are happy with the overall colour and appearance of the chest, you can stop working on it and protect the finish by applying a coat of clear matte and satin polyurethane varnish (mixed together in a ratio of 1:1). Again, apply this with a standard decorator's brush. However, you also have the option of "antiquing" the chest further by toning down the paintwork and faking a subtle accumulation of dust over parts of the surface.

8 Thin a cupful of transparent oil glaze in a ratio of 3:1 with white spirit (mineral spirits). Add a little raw umber and black artist's oils to darken the translucent mixture. Using a standard decorator's brush, apply a thin coat of the tinted glaze over the surface of the chest. Start at the back of one of the sides. If the glaze is too light, add more artist's oils; if it is too dark, dilute it with more transparent oil glaze and white spirit (mineral spirits), mixed in the same ratio as before.

9 While the glaze is still wet, lightly rub it down with grade 00 wire (steel) wool. The aim is to cut back and redistribute the glaze a little so that it does not cover the chest uniformly. The extent to which you alter the glaze is, again, a matter of composition, but generally you will achieve the most realistic finish if you build up darker areas around the drawer knobs, in any recesses, and over the lower half of the chest.

10 Complete step 9 as quickly as possible, so that the glaze is still slightly tacky when you finish. Next, sprinkle a little gray rotten-stone powder onto a pad of lint-free rag. Lightly rub the rag over the the chest, adding more powder when necessary. Some of the powder will cling to the tacky glaze, giving the paintwork a "dusty" appearance. For the most realistic finish, build up the powder on those areas where you would expect to find the greatest accumulation of dust: in the recesses and over horizontal surfaces. Once the underlying glaze has dried, lightly brush off excess powder with a rag. Usually, furniture is protected by putting a mat underneath any water-filled vase placed on top of it. Here, any "bloom" or "bubbling-up" of the paint caused by absorption of moisture simply adds to the authenticity of the finish.

Above and left *The detailed precision of the 19th-century "pattern-box" stencilling on the plank walls of a North American house near Houston, Texas, contrasts with the simpler hand-painted motifs on the beams of an early 20th-century hunting lodge in Norway. (The two-tier cabinet dates from 1768; its fantasy marbling is original.)*

Stencilling & folk art

ONE OF THE MOST NOTABLE CHARACTERISTICS THAT DISTINGUISHES THE INTERIORS *of many country houses from their urban counterparts is the widespread use of stencilling and freehand painting. Implemented by either the home owners themselves, or itinerant artists and craftsmen, these decorative techniques offered a reasonably simple means of embellishing surfaces as diverse as walls, floors, joinery and furniture with colourful motifs, patterns and pictures. Such techniques also provided inexpensive alternatives to the wallpapers, carpets and marquetry work more readily available to wealthier town and city dwellers.*

For thousands of years, stencilling has been one of the easiest, quickest and cheapest means of decorating surfaces with colourful designs. The technique requires minimal artistic skill, and involves transferring a pattern or motif (or a series of them) onto a contrasting-coloured wood, plaster or fabric background by dabbing paints and glazes through cut-outs in a stencil card. During this process, the card is held against, or temporarily fixed to, the underlying surface. Once the card is removed, the pattern or motif is revealed.

Historically, a wide range of paints and glazes have been used for stencilling. Artist's oils, vegetable and mineral dyes, buttermilk or casein-based paints, distemper, metallic paints, water-based emulsions (latex paints), and modern acrylics have all been successfully employed at one time or another. Similarly, decorators have utilized a variety of tools for applying the paints and glazes through the stencil cut-outs – rags, sponges and specialized artists' brushes being among the most popular.

The stencils themselves have been made from materials as diverse as thick sheets of oiled paper or cardboard, thin blocks of wood, and leaves taken from various species of plant. In recent years, stencil kits consisting of pre-cut sheets of clear acetate and artists' acrylic paints have become very popular. However, the most ingenious combination to date is to be found in the

Wall stencilling *in the hallway of a country house in Devon, England. The repeat floral design was copied from a stencilled bedroom at the American Museum in Bath, England. During the 18th and 19th centuries, in the rural areas of North America, Northern Europe and Scandinavia, stencilling provided an inexpensive alternative to hand-printed wallpapers.*

The printed stencil *wallpaper in the hallway of this English country house is one of the many similar examples now available from wallpaper manufacturers, which feature motifs and patterns either copied or inspired by 18th- and 19th-century originals. This paper has been artificially aged with an antiquing glaze.*

Traditional flower-and-leaf *motifs stencilled onto painted lining paper on the walls of a West Country farmhouse in southern England. This traditional stencilling pattern was copied from decorations dated to c.1800 found in Lower Dairy Farm at Little Hocksley in England.*

"Pattern-box" border *stencilling, with stylized floral corner motifs on the colourwashed wooden plank walls of a bedroom in a house in Texas, USA. Like the "spinning stars" scrap quilt on the wooden bed, the decoration dates from around the middle of the 19th century (probably 1840).*

A bedroom at *the American Museum in Bath, England. The hand-stencilled walls, rocking chair and bed cover are typical of those found in North American rural houses during the early years of the 19th century. The repeat flower-and-leaf wall stencilling was done with buttermilk paints.*

Fijian islands, where for many centuries the natives have produced stencilled decorations on a variety of surfaces by brushing locally produced vegetable dyes through the holes made by insects in banana and bamboo leaves.

It is generally accepted that the Chinese invented the art of stencilling around 3000 BC, and used it to decorate papers and silks. The Ancient Egyptians also employed the technique to embellish a wide range of artefacts, including earthenwares and mummy cases. Throughout Europe, during the Middle Ages, stencilled motifs – commonly in the form of rich red, green and gold-coloured heraldic symbols – were often applied to walls of churches, and did much to brighten up their otherwise often gloomy interiors. In medieval France, stencilling was a fashionable means of decorating not only the inside walls of houses, but also textiles, books and manuscripts. In 16th-century England, stencilled wall-hangings (made of hessian) and stencilled limewashed walls could be found in many grander houses in the cities, towns and countryside. From the 14th to the 16th century, the French were even using stencils in the production of prototype, hand-decorated wallpapers. Unfortunately,

Left *The kitchen of an early 19th-century English country cottage. The green-painted brick wall above the door has been augmented with a small stencilled arch of contrasting yellow-gold foliage motifs; the colour echoing the stripped-pine furniture.*

Simple stencilled borders *applied along the tops of the walls and on either side of an open doorway in the kitchen of an English country farmhouse. The position of these flower-and-leaf motif stencils helps to define the architectural features and proportions of the room, while their simple colours relieve the uniform yellow of the colourwashed walls.*

Leaf motif stencils *inspired by traditional stencil designs displayed at the St. Fagan's Folk Art Museum situated near Cardiff in Wales.*

Floral motif stencils *augmented with a hand-painted rope border, add pattern and contrasting colour to the red-oxide-coloured walls of a small galley kitchen, in an 18th-century English house. The owner chose the colour scheme to reflect the fact that the kitchen was converted from part of what was once a chapel.*

A hand-painted bookcase *and a small hand-painted keepbox in a room at "Charleston",
a farmhouse in Sussex, England. During the First World War, the house became a "family"
retreat for the internationally influential writers, artists and designers better known as the
"Bloomsbury Set". They included Vanessa Bell, Duncan Grant and Roger Fry.*

The overmantel decoration *in "The Garden Room" at Charleston was painted c. 1928 by
Duncan Grant. Originally, the two bare-breasted women supported an inset mirror within a
painted oval frame. However, when the mirror broke some years later, Grant initially replaced
it with a yachting scene and, later still, the basket of flowers that survives to this day.*

very few of these have
survived to the present day.

By the end of the 17th
century, and throughout the
18th, the gradual introduction
of hand-painted wallpapers in
Europe, particularly in France
and England, resulted in a
decline in the use of wall-
stencilling in grander urban
households. The development
of mass-produced, printed,
and much more affordable
wallpapers during the 19th
century further exacerbated
this decline. City and town
dwellers of more modest
means could now afford to
emulate their wealthier neigh-
bours, and wallpapered rooms
became *de rigeur* in many
households. Moreover, where
newly fashionable, inexpensive wallpapers were readily
available, employing a decorator to hand-stencil entire walls
became uneconomic.

It would be wrong to give
the impression that stencilling
completely died out in
urban areas during the 19th
century. For example, stencils
were often combined with
wallpapers as simple borders
around the perimeter of a
room, as friezes and cornices,
and at picture- and dado-rail
height. And, in some of the
grander English Regency,
French Empire, and North
American Federal houses of
the 19th century, reception-
room ceilings were sometimes

Right *A detail from the fireplace in
"The Garden Room" at "Charleston"
(shown left). It was constructed by
Bunny Garnett c.1918. The faux stone
effect is augmented by cross-hatching
on the edges of the supports (and on
the overmantel decoration above).*

Folk-painted walls *in a Norwegian hunting lodge built in 1916 in the Hakadal region
north of Oslo. The abstract, hand-painted, cobalt-blue motifs were applied over a paler blue
colourwash. Together with the fantasy blue marble cornice and skirting (baseboard), they
were created by an Italian artist, Dominico Ertmann, in 1917.*

An 18th-century stove *decorated with hand-painted ceramic tiles with blue floral swags-and-tails and borders, in a late 18th-century house in Odenslunda, Sweden. A central urn sits on the overmantel.*

A painted trompe l'oeil *dentil cornice and a floral chain along the frieze decorate the walls in another room from the house shown opposite. Trompe l'oeil architectural fixtures are quite unusual in country interiors.*

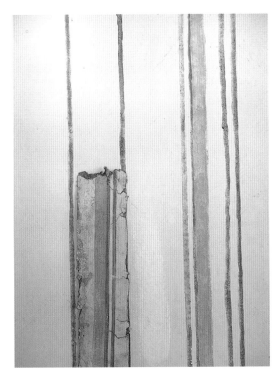

A close-up detail *of the trompe l'oeil picture frame in the room shown above reveals the artistic simplicity associated with trompe l'oeil work in rural areas. Despite this, the work is effective when viewed from a distance.*

The three-dimensional *appearance of the trompe l'oeil cornice shown above is created by brushing on simple lines of darker and lighter shades of paint. However, the effect is lost when viewed close-up.*

decorated with extravagantly stencilled garlands of flowers and fruit, the patterns often trailing down the tops of the walls. Similarly, stencilled wall decoration and furniture enjoyed a revival in more fashion-conscious urban households during the late-19th and early-20th centuries, under the influence of the Arts and Crafts and Art Nouveau movements. Nevertheless, for the vast majority of city dwellers, extensive use of hand-stencilled decorations had become a thing of the past by the end of the 19th century.

However, in rural areas stencilling survived as a much-used and fashionable decorative convention well into the 20th century. Fashion aside, there were technical and economic reasons for this. Firstly, when wallpapers were first introduced, in the 17th and 18th centuries, they were often too expensive or simply unavailable in remoter country areas (such as those in the North American Colonies and large parts of Scandinavia). Secondly, even when cheaper, mass-produced printed wallpapers did become available during the second half of the 19th century, they remained an unsuitable means of decorating wooden and plaster walls that often suffered from seasonal damp. Stencilling, on the other hand, was a technically suitable, and relatively inexpensive, means of imitating the wallpapered interiors of wealthier town and city houses. In addition, when applied to wooden floors

This Norwegian country house, *built between 1796 and 1798, retains original decorations*
that were completed sometime prior to 1820. The blue colourwashed, wooden-plank walls
above the dado have been embellished with a simple trompe l'oeil moulding, intertwined
with a hand-painted floral garland (part of which has not survived).

or cheap canvas floorcloths, it provided an inexpensive alternative to the costly, and often unavailable, patterned carpets that were being increasingly used in urban areas. Apart from the economic considerations, by the end of the 18th century stencilling in rural areas had become established as a respected form of folk art.

Throughout Europe, North America and Scandinavia, folk-art stencilling was largely the preserve of itinerant artists and craftsmen, although some householders did apply their own stencilled decorations. Despite minor regional differences in style, the stencilled patterns and motifs employed in country areas are usually very similar, regardless of location. This is explained by the fact that the majority of itinerant artists and craftsmen who practised the art were of European extraction. For example, in North America most were immigrants from northern Europe and Scandinavia who brought with them ideas on decoration from their place of birth. Thus, for example, the profusion of hand-stencilled motifs and patterns applied to walls, floors, floorcloths, joinery, furniture and artefacts in rural North American Colonial homes is very similar to the extensive and flamboyant use

Folk-painted panels *in a folk-grained door, in the Olen farmhouse in Aludal, Norway (built c.1750). The graining has been extended to the architrave and along the dado, and is bordered by hand-painted floral motifs.*

Hand-painted floral borders *feature in another room in the Olen farmhouse in Aludal, Norway. These decorations, like those shown left, were completed c.1822.*

Right *A bedroom from the house – Sigefstad – shown opposite. Hand-painted floral garlands, intertwined with trompe l'oeil mouldings, are used. The door panels have been hand-painted (Chinese-style) with scenes of a Norwegian harvest.*

of stencilling in many 17th-century Dutch and 18th-century Swedish and Norwegian interiors. Usually applied with buttermilk, or primitive oil-based paints, or distemper, the stencilled motifs and patterns were inspired by nature and the countryside – garlands of flowers, leaves, fruit and berries, and images of native animals and birds were among the most popular.

During the second half of the 19th century, the similarity of stencilled decorations in different countries and regions was further fuelled by the introduction of commercial stencils (or "pattern-box" stencils). Rather than cut his or her own stencils out of materials such as oiled-card, wood and leather, the craftsmen could now purchase pre-cut stencil cards in a range of different sizes and patterns and motifs. However, to partly overcome the element of uniformity that commercial stencils introduced to the art, individual artists and craftsmen often augmented the patterns and motifs. This was done with highlights, shading and small hand-painted details after the stencil card had been removed.

The element of individuality that each painter brought to his work is much more

Left *The seaborn trading links between China and Norway during the early 19th century are reflected in these Chinese-style hand-painted door panels in a bedroom of the Norwegian house, Sigefstad, also shown on pages 74–5.*

The painted wooden plank walls *of a bedroom in Aset – a late-18th-century Norwegian country mansion in the Osterdalen region – are embellished with a simple stencilled floral motif. The sophisticated, folk-painted drawer-fronts of the desk show scenes copied during the early years of the 19th century by the artist Sjolie, from an imported French tapestry.*

A painted armoire *decorated c.1822 in the Olen farmhouse, Norway. As well as a folk-grained carcass and a faux marble cornice, the armoire incorporates folk-painted panels depicting rustic scenes and abstract motifs. The side chair next to it has also been fantasy wood-grained.*

This large cupboard *decorated in 1744 by a Swedish artist resides in Synvis-stua – a large country house built in 1668 in the Oslo region of Norway. The lower portion of the cupboard has been folk-grained, and features "pebble-marbled" panels in the carcass, and a folk-painted door panel.*

An 18th-century folk-painted chest of drawers, seen through a doorway in the Olen
farmhouse in Aludal, Norway. Decorated c.1822, the chest features hand-painted floral
motifs on the drawer-fronts, which echo the painted floral borders along the walls and
around the door in the foreground.

Left *A painted grandfather clock, dated 1777, in an early 19th-century hunting lodge in the Hakadal region north of Oslo, Norway. In addition to the hand-painted inscription, there are nautical motifs above the clockface and stylized insect motifs on the base of the case. Other forms of decoration include fantasy blue marbling around the face, the inscription, and the plinth, together with painted gilding (on the pillars flanking the face).*

A detail of the *Danish table at Aas Gard (shown right). Dated to c.1750, it has been hand-painted with flowing, Scandinavian Rococo flower-and-leaf motifs. (The inset tabletop is faience.)*

Stencilled, German-spruce *wall-panelling, sent to Italy for decoration and installed in a room at Aas Gard, a Norwegian country house (built before 1750 and redecorated in 1852). The painting on the wall is of Thomas Fearnley, an artist friend of the renowned English painter, Turner. The table is of Danish origin.*

A large pine *cupboard from the Uppland region of Sweden. Dated to 1774, its door panels and cornice have been decorated with hand-painted roses. The upper panels are framed with rustic marbling.*

A folk-grained *19th-century wardrobe. The cross-hatched pattern painted on the door panels may well have been intended as an amusing simulation of the wire-mesh found in country pie safes of the period.*

A 19th-century *carved and folk-painted bed at the Mora farm, in a remote part of Sweden. As in most Scandinavian country areas, the farmer would have paid an itinerant painter to decorate the bed.*

This folk-painted wardrobe *originates from southern Germany. As is clear from the painted panel on one of the doors, it was decorated at the end of the 18th century. The style of decoration is very similar to that found on Pennsylvanian pieces from the same period. This is due to the fact that many of the itinerant painters in North America were of German origin.*

apparent in another important decorative tradition that has been practised for centuries in country homes. In Europe, folk painting has its roots in the hand-painted murals and motifs used to decorate the interior walls of churches during the Middle Ages. Often practised by the same itinerant craftsmen who applied stencilled decorations, it had spread to even the humblest of country households by the beginning of the 18th century. Throughout the 18th and 19th centuries, in the rural areas of Europe, North America and Scandinavia, it remained a fashionable alternative, or accompaniment, to stencilling, and is still sometimes used to this day.

Over the centuries, folk art has appeared in a number of guises. At its most sophisticated, it can be described as provincial fine art of the highest quality. Many of the finest examples are to be found in Scandinavia, where the walls of some of the rooms in grander country homes are covered in pictorial decoration depicting religious, historical or rustic scenes. Although less formal, the quality of the work would not look out of place in the Renaissance churches and palaces of Rome, Florence and Venice, in Italy.

A 19th-century provincial *chest-of-drawers in a house in Provence, southern France. Applied on top of a green background, the red and gold painted edges and fronts of the drawers define the shape and proportions of the piece.*

A folk-painted cupboard *in a country house in the French alps. The rustic floral and animal motifs are typical of the painted decorations found on European alpine furniture, and would have been done by an itinerant artist.*

Right *While numerous examples of folk-painting are quite sophisticated representations of rural scenes and motifs, there are just as many instances of very simple and naive forms of decoration. Here, simple mono-colour circles and cross-hatching decorate the 18th-century, French wall-hung corner cupboard.*

An early 19th-century *Norwegian baby's wooden cradle. The exterior of this hanging cradle is painted in a washed-out cobalt blue; the four corners are embellished with hand-painted roses. Of all the floral motifs used to decorate furniture in Scandinavian countries during the 18th and 19th centuries, the rose was consistently the most popular.*

A wooden storage bucket, *from an early 20th-century hunting lodge situated in the Hakadal region north of Oslo, Norway. The colourfully depicted fruit-and-foliage motifs are typical of the hand-painted decorations found on storage vessels and other items of kitchenalia found throughout this region.*

A painted, woven *wooden trug or basket – one of a number of items representing the rich tradition of handicrafts associated with the remote, afforested Mora region of Sweden.*

A 19th-century *steamed-wood container. Items such as this are usually made in rural communities from birch, maple or cherrywood, and often hand-painted or stencilled with rustic motifs.*

A North American *19th-century Shaker-style box. Made by steaming and interleaving thin strips of wood, the oval box was then painted with a blue basecoat, and finished with a floral motif.*

The tradition of folk painting *in country areas has survived the encroachment of mass-produced furniture and utensils during the 20th century. This modern hand-turned wooden bowl from North America has been patriotically hand-painted with the Stars and Stripes.*

A Mexican drum *in blue-painted wood sits on a large pine trunk in a Santa Fé house in New Mexico. The local painter has naively depicted a dog chasing a frightened Mexican peasant around the sides of the drum. The style of the work strongly reflects the influence of Native American art in the region.*

A North American *rocking chair. Made from cut branches and twigs (some of which have been steamed into shape), it is very much a country piece, and intended for use out of doors. Perhaps it was the maker's intention, but it is difficult to know whether to attribute the "painted" decoration to man or bird.*

This ornate bird cage *is North American and subtly patriotic—the front, sides and back of the wooden frame have been painted red, white and blue. The national flag is symbolized by the overlay of contrasting-coloured, painted stars, and the (vertical) stripes of the metal cage bars.*

In addition to this mural work, it is not unusual to find exquisitely hand-painted pieces of furniture, embellished with colourful and decorative motifs – flora and fauna being the most popular subject matter. Of particular note is the *rosmålning* (or rose-painting) tradition of Norway and Sweden. Fashionable from the start of the 18th century to the beginning of the 20th, it involves the depiction of intertwined roses and acanthus-like leaves – the latter inspired by Classical decorative motifs. Applied to walls (often in the form of panels or borders) and furniture, *rosmålning* has a vibrancy and fluency of style not matched by flower-and-leaf stencilled motifs.

The standard of folk painting was dependant upon the artistic abilities of the decorator. Given that many country householders without artistic training also took up a brush, it is not unusual to find much simpler examples of the art. Where someone has bitten off more than they can chew, the results can be embarrassingly crude. On the other hand, easily hand-painted motifs, such as stars and hearts, lend country interiors and furniture a naive charm often absent in sophisticated urban houses.

Left *This rustic, early 19th-century North American checkers board represents folk painting in its simplest and most functional form. The hand-painted squares facilitate the playing of the game when the board is in use, and introduce a decorative pattern to a room when the board is hung up.*

Border stencil

The fleur-de-lis stencil motif used in this project was traced from non-copyright reference material, transferred to a sheet of stencil card (available from most good craft stores), and cut out with a scalpel blade. If you wish to change the size of a stencil motif you can do this by photocopying the original design (on a machine with an enlarging and reducing facility), and then tracing the copy onto the card. If you feel confident in your artistic abilities, you could omit the tracing stage and simply draw the motif freehand onto the card.

WHAT YOU NEED

Reference material A photograph, drawing or print of the motif that you wish to copy.

Tracing paper For copying the outline of the stencil from source material.

Masking tape (optional). For securing the stencil card onto the wall.

HB pencil Use to trace the outline of the stencil and transfer to stencil card.

Graphite stick Use to shade over the traced outline of the stencil prior to transferring to stencil card.

Stencil card Use this for cutting out the stencil design.

Cutting board For supporting the stencil card when cutting out the design.

Craft knife Use this, or a scalpel blade, to cut out the stencil card.

Ruler Use to establish the position of the stencil in relation to the ceiling.

Spirit level For establishing a true horizontal line for the border around the walls.

Small mixing containers You will need one or two containers – 1 litre (1¾ UK pint/ 1 US quart) – for mixing the stencil glaze.

Transparent oil (scumble) glaze No more than 0.5 litre (1 UK pint/½ US quart) will be required for a border around an average-size room.

White spirit (mineral spirits) You will need a small bottle.

Artist's oil One small tube of burnt umber.

Bronze metallic powder You will need a small pot.

Step ladder For reaching the area of wall that you are stencilling.

Stencil brush Medium-sized, stiff-bristled brush.

Lining paper For dabbing off excess glaze from the bristles of the stencil brush.

Sandpaper Use a medium-grade (grit) paper for cutting back and artificially ageing the stencilled motif.

Eraser When you have finished, use this to rub out the faint pencil line marking the position of the stencil around the walls.

1 Place the reference material containing the motif you wish to copy face-up on a flat work surface. Cover it with a sheet of tracing paper, securing the corners of the paper to the work surface with short strips of masking tape. Then, using an HB pencil, trace around the outline of the motif. Note: A smaller motif, designed to alternate with the main motif around the border was also traced, but you can omit this if you wish.

2 Peel off the masking tape, lift up the tracing paper and remove the reference material. Turn the tracing paper over so that the pencil outlines are face-down on the work surface. Then, using a graphite stick, shade over the back of the outlined motifs with diagonal, overlapping strokes. Do not leave any areas uncovered or the designs will not transfer completely to the card at the next stage.

3 Tape some stencil card – about 30cm (1ft) long by 20cm (8in) wide – to the work surface. Tape the tracing paper over the card, with the shading underneath and the larger motif near the right end. Pencil firmly around the outline. Remove the paper to reveal the outline on the card. Repeat across the card, alternating equally spaced small and large motifs, and finishing with the right half of a large motif on the left edge.

4 If necessary, pencil over the outlines once more, and then remove the strips of masking tape securing the card to the work surface. Place the card on a cutting board and use a craft knife or scalpel blade to carefully cut out the sections of card that lie within the outlines of the larger and smaller motifs. To reduce the risk of the blade slipping when cutting around a curve you should slowly turn the card around the blade, rather than the blade around the card.

5 Stand well back from the wall and establish a suitable height for the border. Using a ruler and pencil, make a faint mark on the wall to establish the position of the bottom of the stencil card. Starting from this point, work your way around the walls with a long spirit level and a pencil, making a faint pencil line as you go. This will establish a true horizontal for the stencil, and ensure that when you return to the point at which you started the lines will join up.

6 Start at the left end of the wall. Align the card with the pencil mark and secure corners with tape. Mix a glaze: 40 percent transparent oil glaze; 20 percent white spirit (mineral spirits); 20 percent burnt umber artist's oil; 20 percent bronze metallic powder. For an average room you will need 0.25 litre (¼ UK pint/1 US cup) of glaze. Dip the bristles of a stencil brush in the glaze, dab off excess on lining paper, and pounce the bristles up and down over the stencil cut-outs.

7 Once you have dabbed the glaze over all the cut-outs, peel off the masking tape and lift the card off the wall. Do not drag it off, or you may smear the drying glaze. With a cotton rag, wipe off any glaze that has seeped onto the back of the card. Move to the right and re-position the card on the pencil line, so that the half cut-out of the larger motif on the left edge sits exactly over the right half of the last motif that you stencilled in step 6.

8 Repeat steps 6 and 7 all the way around the wall. To achieve the right spacing between the last and first motif of the perimeter, you may need to make some minor adjustments to the position of the card as you work your way along the final wall. Do this by moving the card slightly to the left or right, as required. Small changes to the spaces between seven or eight motifs will not be noticed, unlike a particularly large or small space between the first and last motif.

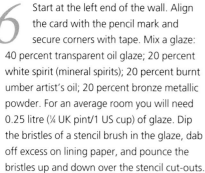

9 Once you have removed the card for the final time, you can leave the stencil as it is (as shown above). Alternatively, you can artificially age the motifs by rubbing them down with a medium-grade (grit) sandpaper once the glaze has dried (after about 36 hours). Lightly rub in all directions over the motifs, changing the sandpaper as and when necessary, and making sure that you do not remove any of the background wall finish.

10 Cutting back and fading the glaze with sandpaper produces a finish similar in appearance to old stucco work. This involved painting pictures and motifs onto wet plaster; over time the pigments in the glazes faded, and the plaster became unstable and chipped off in places, giving the decoration an aesthetically pleasing distressed appearance. Finally, rub out any remaining faint pencil lines with an eraser.

Stencilled floorcloth

Before the advent of mass-produced carpets during the late 19th century, floorcloths provided an inexpensive means of covering bare wooden floorboards. Floorcloths were particularly popular in North America and Britain – commonly found in rural areas. Usually made of heavyweight canvas, they were stiffened and primed with a varnish and then painted or stencilled with motifs and patterns. You can buy pre-cut stencils in traditional designs from craft stores and specialist suppliers. Alternatively, you can cut your own stencils.

WHAT YOU NEED

Dust sheet (or sheets of newspaper).

Heavyweight canvas Pre-primed for painting.

Steel ruler Use when cutting down canvas.

Craft knife A heavy-duty type.

Milk paints About 0.25 litres (¼ UK pint/1 US cup) of pale yellow for the basecoat. Half that for the following stencil colours: rust-red, mid-green, mid-blue and bright yellow.

Standard decorator's brushes You will need two 5cm (2½in) brushes for applying the basecoat and protective glaze.

Tracing paper Two large sheets.

HB pencil For tracing outline of stencil.

Graphite stick For shading over traced outline.

Stencil card Two or three large sheets.

Masking tape For securing the stencil.

Stencil brushes A selection of different sizes.

White matte emulsion (latex) paint You will need about 0.25 litres (¼ UK pint/1 US cup).

Acrylic scumble glaze Less than 0.25 litres (¼ UK pint/1 US cup) for a protective finish.

Mixing containers Five 1 litre (1¾ UK pints/1 US quart) plastic or metal pots for mixing paints and glazes.

Lint-free rag For cleaning stencil card

1 Purchase some pre-sized ready-primed canvas from a specialist fabric supplier. If necessary, cut down the canvas to the required dimensions with a steel ruler and a heavy-duty craft knife. (There is no need to oversew or bind the edges.) Lay the canvas flat on a dust sheet (or sheets of newspaper) and brush on two coats of a pale yellow milk paint with a standard decorator's brush. This will serve as the basecoat for the stencil. Depending on room temperature and humidity, you should allow about 4 hours' drying time after each coat.

2 If you are cutting your own stencil, use the technique described on pages 90–1. Alternatively, buy a pre-cut stencil of a suitable size. You will need one stencil for the border and one for the central motif. Starting with the border, work out the position of the pattern repeat and, beginning at a corner, secure the stencil with masking tape. Using stencil brushes of a suitable size, dab on the paints and glazes (specified in step 4 below) through the cut-outs. However, you should dab off excess glaze from the bristles onto spare paper before applying.

3 When you have completed one side of the border, turn the corner and realign the stencil along the adjacent edge. In this example the stencil repeat was established by always positioning the trailing edge of the foliage the same distance from the large flower motif at the other end of the stencil. Each time you complete a section wipe off any paint from the underside of the card with lint-free rag. This will ensure that no smudges of paint are transferred to the floorcloth.

4 On completing the border, measure and mark the middle of the floorcloth with a pencil. Tape the central motif stencil in position and apply the colours as before. For both the border and central motifs just four colours were used: rust-red milk paint; 60 percent mid-blue milk paint mixed with 40 percent white matte emulsion (latex); 75 percent mid-green milk paint mixed with 25 percent white matte emulsion (latex); and bright yellow milk paint.

5 When you have finished the stencilling, leave it to dry for about 12 hours. If you are satisfied with the colours, simply apply a protective coat of matte finish acrylic scumble glaze (emulsion or latex glaze) over the surface of the floorcloth, using a standard decorator's brush. If you wish to tone down the colours and give the cloth a slightly dusty, "aged" appearance (as here), tint the glaze as follows: 80 percent acrylic scumble to 20 percent matte white emulsion (latex) paint.

Stencilled box

The American folk-art stencil shown here is just one example from a wide range of traditional European, Scandinavian and American stencils now available from specialist suppliers (see pages 170–3). If you need to adjust the size of the stencil to fit the dimensions of the object that you wish to decorate, simply increase or decrease it by an appropriate percentage on a photocopier. Then, using a pencil and graphite stick, trace the photocopy onto a blank stencil card and carefully remove the cut-outs with a scalpel blade.

WHAT YOU NEED

Folk art stencil kit (fruit and foliage). Plus, if you need to adjust the stencil size: stencil card, scalpel, graphite stick, tracing paper, and access to a photocopier.

Lint-free rag To clean box.

White spirit (mineral spirits) To clean box.

Sandpaper (medium-grade/grit). Loose sheets of sandpaper (rather than sandpaper blocks) are more convenient for awkward areas.

Primer/undercoat (optional). If working on bare wood.

Spare paper For dabbing off any excess paint.

Paints Dark green, bright red, mid-yellow and mid-blue milk paint. Plus black and white artist's powder pigments.

Brushes Three small artist's brushes, a 5cm (2in) standard decorator's brush, and a soft-bristled varnishing brush.

Artist's palette (or white laminated card).

Masking tape The "low-tack" type will minimize the risk of lifting paint from the surface to which the tape is attached.

Clear polyurethane varnish Use a matte or satin (mid-sheen) finish. If desired, the higher sheen of the latter can be "knocked back" by mixing it in a ratio of 1:1 with the former.

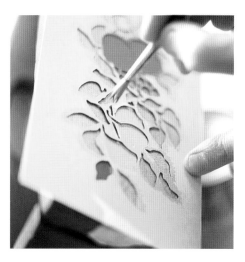

1 Remove any dirt, wax or grease from the surface of the box by rubbing it down with a lint-free rag dipped in white spirit (mineral spirits). If the box has been painted or varnished, key the surface by rubbing it down with medium-grade (grit) sandpaper. (On bare wood, apply a coat of primer/undercoat.) When the surface is clean and dry, apply two coats of dark green milk paint with a standard decorator's brush. Allow each coat to dry for 12 hours before applying the next.

2 Secure the stencil along one side of the box with masking tape. Charge a small artist's brush with red milk paint, and dab off any excess on a spare piece of paper. Fill in the red fruits by lightly pouncing the tips of the bristles through the stencil cut-outs. Do not overload the brush, and gradually build up the colour. Next, darken the blue milk paint with a little black artist's powder pigment, and fill in the small berries. Repeat for the other fruits using yellow milk paint.

3 Mix a small amount of white artist's powder pigment with water. Gradually add it to some of the dark green milk paint that you used for the basecoat applied in step 1. Keep adding a little more of the white pigment until you have lightened the green enough to achieve a sufficient contrast against the darker background colour. Then, again using a small artist's brush, pounce the light green paint through the stencil cut-outs for the leaves.

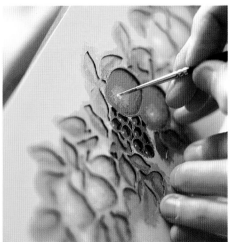

4 At this stage you can remove the stencil to reveal an attractive motif that can simply be repeated on the other sides of the box. As an additional touch, you can achieve a more impressive and professional-looking result by adding highlights and shadows to the fruit and foliage. To do this, mix some white and then some black artist's powder pigments with water. Gradually incorporate a little of each into the original colours, adding white to lighten and black to darken.

5 On each fruit, berry and leaf, establish the position from which the dominant light source will strike: in this case, toward the top left-hand side. Then, using a fine-pointed artist's brush, carefully paint on the lighter versions of the colours to create highlights on those areas most exposed to the light source. Repeat with the darkened colours to create shadows on those areas of the fruit, berries and leaves least exposed to the light (such as recesses in the leaves).

6 Once the paint has dried, carefully remove the stencil card to reveal the finished motif. Then repeat steps 2–5 on the other three sides of the box. Although milk paint is fairly hard-wearing, it is advisable to apply a coat of varnish to protect the finish, particularly if it will be exposed to moisture. Use either clear matte polyurethane varnish, or mix the matte with satin (mid-sheen) finish varnish in a ratio of 1:1. The latter will create a subtle lustre across the surface of the box.

Folk-painted cupboard

The tradition of decorating pieces of furniture and other joinery with freehand-painted pictures, patterns and motifs (folk painting) is centuries old, and prevalent in many of the rural communities of Europe (particularly Scandinavia) and North America. The primary purpose of folk painting was to introduce colour and pattern into the house, and embellish bland-looking softwoods that had little or no figuring or grain. Examples range from the simple to the sophisticated, and reflect the artistic abilities of the painter.

WHAT YOU NEED

Standard decorator's brushes You will need two 5cm (2in) brushes for the undercoat and basecoat, one 7.5cm (3in) for the antiquing glaze, and one 2.5cm (1in) for painting the door and frames.

White primer/undercoat For sealing and preparing the bare wood.

Matte white emulsion (latex) paint Use to lighten the basecoat.

Mixing containers Five or six old glass (jam) jars will be sufficient.

Milk paints Mid-yellow for the basecoat, rust-red for the door and carcass frames.

HB pencil For sketching the design.

Sheets of lining paper As above.

Artist's acrylic paints You need to buy small tubes of red, yellow, green, blue, black and white.

Artist's palette For mixing paints and glazes.

Artist's brushes Have a selection of small, fine-bristled ones – sable bristles are best for freehand painting.

Acrylic scumble glaze Also known as emulsion (latex) glaze.

Raw umber universal stainer For tinting the scumble glaze.

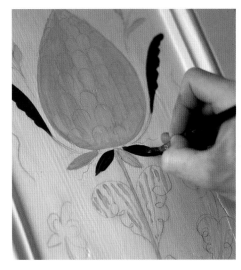

1 Whether the cupboard is bare wood or already painted, prepare the surface for decoration as described on pages 167–8. Next, using a standard decorator's brush, apply two coats of white primer/undercoat. Allow to dry for about 8 hours after each coat. Then apply two coats of a pale yellow basecoat. In this case a mid-yellow milk paint was mixed half-and-half with matte white emulsion (latex) paint.

2 Sketch out the intended design first on a spare piece of lining paper. This will allow you to make any necessary adjustments without having to reapply the basecoat applied in step 1. If you do not wish to produce your own design, trace one from some reference material, transfer it to the lining paper and adapt it freehand. When you are satisfied with the design, reproduce the pattern on the cupboard, using an HB pencil.

3 Mix the artist's acrylics on a palette or in small containers, slightly diluting them with water. How much water you add is a matter of trial and error: the more you add, the more translucent the colour. You can also experiment with mixing colours in varying proportions to either change them completely or to adjust their tone. Then, using a selection of small artist's brushes, gradually build up the background colours of the design.

4 Let the background colours dry for at least 4 hours. Then apply the fine details, again using small, fine-bristled artist's brushes. The amount of detail that you add is a matter of composition and personal choice. However, you will find that many objects, such as fruit and flowers, will have more definition if they are outlined with a border of tiny motifs (which can be as simple as a series of small dots).

5 When you have completed the motifs on the door and side panels, step back and assess the overall appearance of the cupboard. With this example, it was felt that the cupboard had a rather pleasing shape, and that this could be beneficially defined by picking out the the frames of the door and side panels with two coats of rust-red milk paint. Leave to dry for about 4–6 hours after each coat.

6 If you are satisfied with the brightness of the colours, finish by applying a coat of acrylic scumble glaze (emulsion/latex glaze) with a standard decorator's brush. However, if you want to tone down the colours and "age" the finish, brush on one or two coats of an antiquing glaze consisting of 90 percent acrylic scumble and 10 percent raw umber universal stainer. Leave to dry for about 2–4 hours after each coat.

Above and left *Many examples of faux marble found in urban houses are accurate simulations of real stone. In country areas, however, "fantasy" marbling was more typical: witness the door, architrave, and built-in bed of a Norwegian hunting lodge, on which marble veins are only loosely suggested, and colours bear little relation to reality.*

Rustic stone effects

THE TECHNIQUE OF USING PAINTS AND GLAZES TO SIMULATE THE COLOURS, patterns and textures of decorative stonework on everything from walls to furniture has been practised for thousands of years. The popularity of replicating cut and polished metamorphic rocks (such as marble) and igneous rocks (such as porphyry) with inexpensive paints and glazes developed because of the lack of availability of stone in many areas, the difficulty in transporting it over long distances (especially to remote country areas), and its often prohibitive cost.

Decorative stones such as marble, porphyry and granite have been among the most prestigious of building materials since Classical Greek and Roman times. Capable of being polished to a subtle, lustrous sheen, and characterized by colourful mineral deposits (such as opal, quartz and turquoise) that lie on or just below their surfaces, such stones instantly convey impressions of solidity, style and affluence whenever they are used.

Unfortunately, these decorative stones – which are quarried from metamorphic and igneous rock – are only found in sizeable quantities in certain parts of the world, most notably in Italy, France and Belgium. This fact, along with the high cost of quarrying, cutting, polishing, and transporting them over long distances, has tended to restrict their use to wealthier clients and grander civic and residential buildings – the majority of which are located in cities and large towns, rather than in the countryside.

Various technical factors have also restricted the use of marble, porphyry and granite as building materials. Because of their density and weight, they perform well under compression – in block form they are ideal for building columns and walls, as thick slabs they are suitable for flooring, and as thin veneers they can be used for wall cladding. However, their density and weight makes them perform badly under tension. In other words, they snap or crack if used for ceilings, overhangs or beams.

A "pebble-marbled" door panel, *part of a cabinet at the Hansmoen farmhouse, built c.1700 in the mountainous region of Tynset, Norway. The cabinet was made c.1739 in the Norwegian baroque style, and painted c.1836. It also features a faux marble cornice, and faux marble panels in the sides of the carcass.*

Furniture and joinery *at the Hansmoen farmhouse in Norway was marbled during the decorations of c.1836. Following the extensive use of marbling in Scandinavian churches during the 17th century, the finish rapidly became a status symbol in both country and urban houses.*

Sienna marbling *on the door, skirting (base) board and bed, in a bedroom of an early 20th-century Norwegian hunting lodge. Much of the 19th- and 20th-century marbling in Scandinavia is a more accurate simulation of the real stone than the generally impressionistic examples of the 17th and 18th centuries.*

Faux marbled beams *in the dining room of the same Norwegian hunting lodge as the bedroom shown above right. This is certainly fantasy marbling because the structural properties of real marble, which performs well under compression but poorly under tension, negate its use for overhead beams.*

Marbling in detail, *on the tops of the walls and ceiling in a room in the hunting lodge shown left and above. The faux marble wall panels are echoed in the panelled inserts between the beams above. As with the beams (left), real marble is rarely used for ceilings and overhangs as it usually cracks under the tension.*

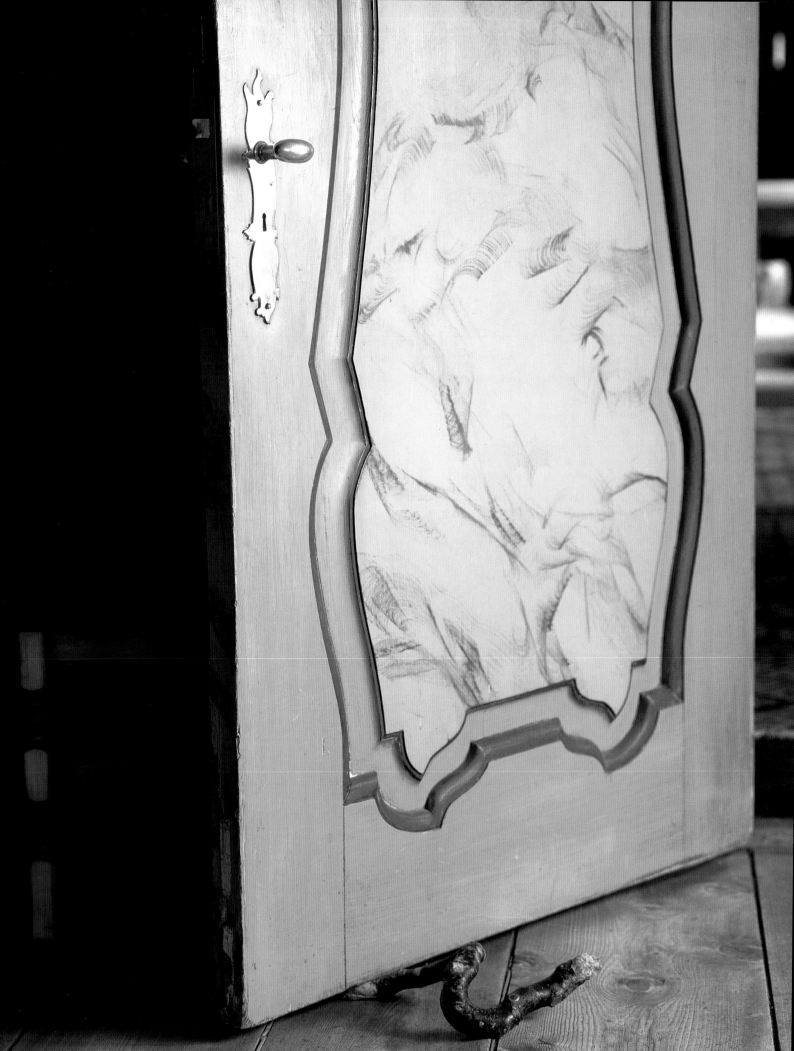

Therefore, lack of availability, high cost and structural limitations have restricted the use of marble, porphyry and granite. So it is not at all surprising that artists and decorators have, for centuries, been called upon to simulate them using paints and glazes. For example, faux porphyry has been found on walls in the ruins of the ancient Roman city of Pompeii, in Italy. Faux marble also appears on many surfaces in large houses built in Italy and France during the Renaissance (and thereafter). Faux marble and porphyry wall panelling, plasterwork, columns and joinery are also a feature of grander, classically inspired, English and North American houses of the 18th and, particularly, the 19th centuries. Indeed, in many 19th-century English and North American houses it was not unusual to find entire rooms decorated in faux marble.

As the quality of paints and glazes improved, and painters and decorators became more technically sophisticated, the standard of these painted illusions developed accordingly, to a point where, notably in England during the 19th century, they were often indistinguishable from the real thing. For example, English artists Thomas Kershaw

Left *A detail of a door panel shown in the room above. The faux marbling in this hunting lodge was done by an Italian artist, Dominico Ertmann, in 1917. The style is in keeping with the tradition of rustic "farmer marbling" of the previous three centuries.*

A Norwegian salon *in the hunting lodge shown on pages 102–3. The traditional cobalt-blue glaze used for marbling in many areas of Scandinavia is seen here on the door and wall panels, and has also been utilized to provide a complementary colourwash on the walls, ceiling beams and the architrave around the doors.*

Realistic veining patterns *on this faux-marbled door reveal the more naturalistic style adopted in Scandinavia during the 20th century.*

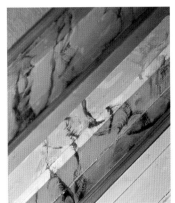

Alternatives to cobalt-blue, *predominant in Norwegian marbling. Here black and yellow is used for a fantasy yellow Sienna marble.*

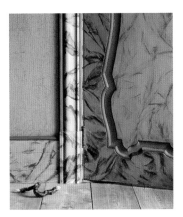

A cobalt-blue marbled *door panel contrasts with the yellow and black veined marble (as left) on the surrounding woodwork.*

and John Taylor produced facsimiles of reddish-orange porphyries, and green serpentine, red levanto and yellow sienna marbles, that maintained the illusion even under the closest scrutiny.

However, the tradition of producing sophisticated and accurate simulations of decorative stonework was, like the use of real decorative stonework, largely confined to civic buildings and grander urban residential houses. In country areas a cruder and more naive style of faux stonework was practised. In such work the painted illusion often bore little resemblance to the real stone – colours and veining were sometimes flights-of-fantasy on the part of the artist or painter. This stylized approach is evident in the faux marbling found in many North American rural homes of the 18th and 19th centuries. Mostly produced by itinerant craftsmen of European origin, it is often gaudily coloured and opaquely patterned, and displays none of the accurate configuration of veins and subtle translucency and depths of realistic colour found in, for example, Thomas Kershaw's and John Taylor's work in Victorian England.

One of the main explana-tions for this lack of accuracy in many examples of country

The upper hallway *of a Norwegian hunting lodge north of Oslo. The bold, abstract fantasy marbling on the walls contrasts with the more conventional cobalt-blue marbling in the bedroom beyond. The door panel is folk-grained in pine.*

marbling is the fact that the itinerant artist or painter often worked without any reference material to hand. This was the case during the 17th and 18th centuries where, in some areas, many itinerant decorators would have never even seen a piece of real marble – their visual reference was limited to, and distorted by, a fellow craftsman's own naive experiments. This is not to say, however, that the end product was without artistic or decorative merit. Indeed, numerous examples of country marbling have a spontaneity and exuberance that suggests or implies, rather than emphatically states, the illusion – and, from the late 18th-century onward, often quite deliberately so.

The tradition of stylized fantasy marbling (and other similarly painted stone effects) is at its strongest in the rural areas of Sweden and Norway. *Faux* marbling first appeared in Scandinavia in Swedish churches during the 16th century. By the 17th century it had spread, via itinerant peasant craftsmen, to the farms and cottages of southern Sweden. The rising popularity of what became known as "farmer marbling" was fuelled by farmers and rural householders keen to decorate their homes with colourful and prestigious finishes that emulated the grander interiors found in many city and town houses. Such a statement of style and wealth was further underlined by the fact that the homeowner was obviously able to afford the services of a specialist painter.

Scandinavian rustic marbling *from the 17th, 18th and 19th centuries was often produced by painters or householders who had never actually seen a genuine piece of marble. Accurate simulations were therefore hard to find. This early 20th-century example indicates that the painter had access to reference material.*

Woodwork and furniture *in this Norwegian country bedroom are decorated in orange and yellow faux marble. This scheme is also echoed on the skirting (base) board.*

"Heaven beds" *(or* himmel seng *beds) are a common feature of Norwegian country homes. Comfortable, often built-in, and decoratively carved, they are usually folk-grained, hand-painted, or marbled (as here).*

By the late 18th century, strident, and predominantly non-naturalistic faux marble finishes were being applied to walls, ceilings, joinery and pieces of furniture (notably beds) in numerous households in rural Sweden and Norway. This decorative tradition was to survive well into the 20th century. It is interesting to note that numerous examples of Scandinavian, and especially Norwegian, faux marbling are predominantly blue in colour. The main reason for this is the fact that Norway mined and exported large quantities of cobalt, notably to China (where it was used in the decoration of blue and white Chinese ceramics). Cobalt was thus in abundant supply to Scandinavian painters who, like itinerant craftsmen in North America and Europe, tinted most of their paints and glazes with locally available pigments.

Throughout Scandinavia, the popularity of marbling as a decorative convention was only matched by *Stenkmålning* (or "spatter-painting"), a technique that involved flicking small spots of different coloured glazes from the bristles of a brush over walls and other surfaces. Sensitively done, it enabled the painter to produce accurate simulations of porphyries and granites. However, in many country areas the paints and glazes were spattered on with a bunch of birch twigs – producing results closer to an abstract painting than a piece of real porphyry or granite – but decoratively no less dramatic and effective.

Most himmel seng beds *have a built-under storage facility. As is the case with the example above right, the veining patterns of the marbling make no concession to the separate construction of the drawer and the carcass.*

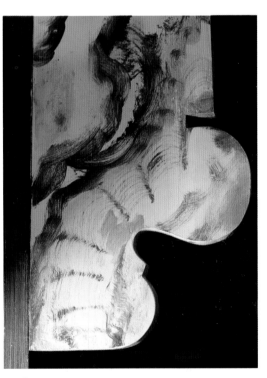

A fantasy marble detail *of the carved* himmel seng *bed shown left. This example dates from the second decade of the 20th century, but in a style that has remained consistently fashionable in rural areas since the 17th century.*

Marbled mantelpiece

Marbling can be divided into two basic types: painted simulations that replicate a particular variety of marble, and painted simulations that are a pastiche of marble. Rustic or "country" marbling usually falls into the latter category, in the sense that while the finish is inspired by the overall appearance of marble – colours and patterns formed by mineral deposits that lie on and just below the surface of the stone – no specific marble is being represented. This offers considerable artistic licence to the painter.

WHAT YOU NEED

Dust sheet For protecting the floor.

Masking tape To protect the cast-iron insert, tiles and surrounding walls.

Mixing containers Have four or five plastic or metal containers, each with a capacity of about 2 litres (3½ UK pints/2 US quarts).

Lint-free rag For cleaning brushes, mopping up spills and buffing the polish.

Standard decorator's brushes Four would be preferable: one for each of the three basic marbling glazes, and one for applying the protective acrylic scumble (emulsion/latex) glaze. You will find that 5cm (2in) brushes are best.

Artist's brushes Buy a small brush with a pointed tip, and a 6mm (¼in) artist's fitch, for applying the veins.

Primer/undercoat You need about ½ litre (1 UK pint/½ US quart) of a white oil-based type to cover an average-size mantelpiece.

White matte emulsion (latex) paint About ½ litre (1 UK pint/½ US quart).

Universal stainers Small tubes of black, raw umber, burnt umber, burnt sienna, and yellow ochre.

Emulsion (latex) glaze You will need about ½ litre (1 UK pint/½ US quart) for protecting the finish.

Furniture polish Tinted or clear wax.

1 Mix in advance the following three glazes (you will need about 0.25 litres/½ UK pint/¼ US quart of each): **A:** 30 percent white matte emulsion (latex) paint, and 70 percent raw umber universal stainer. **B:** 30 percent white matte emulsion (latex) paint, 40 percent burnt umber stainer, and 30 percent burnt sienna stainer. **C:** 30 percent white matte emulsion (latex) paint, 40 percent black stainer, and 30 percent raw umber stainer.

2 Mask off the surrounding areas and apply two coats of white primer/undercoat to the mantelpiece. Leave to dry, then brush on two coats of 30 percent white matte emulsion (latex), 40 percent black stainer, 30 percent raw umber stainer. After these basecoats have dried, use a standard decorator's brush to start applying glaze **A** to the frieze of the mantelpiece. Try to create an uneven, cloud-like shape over a small area.

3 Without delay, dip a second standard decorator's brush into glaze **B**, and apply as before. You should aim to cover an adjacent (and similar-sized and shaped) area to glaze **A**. However, you also want to overlap the two glazes slightly. You can even apply small blotches of glaze **B** in the middle of glaze **A**. This is a matter of personal taste, although you will obviously find it helpful to use the illustration for guidance.

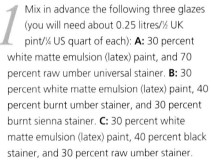

4 Again working as quickly as possible, dip a third standard decorator's brush into glaze **C**, and apply as before. It is now a matter of dipping alternately into the three glazes as you work your way across the frieze of the mantelpiece. You should note that additional subtle variations in colour can be produced by applying sections of glaze **C** with one, or both, of the brushes you used for glazes **A** and **B**. Once you have finished the frieze, move on to another section – in this case, the frieze was followed by the vertical surrounds and sides, and, finally, the mantel shelf. Remember to overlap glazes slightly so they are not too sharply defined.

5 Having finished the background colours, leave the surface to dry thoroughly for up to 6 hours. Next, mix an off-white glaze. This is used to simulate the veins that run across and through the surface of the majority of marbles. The veining glaze should consist of 80 percent white matte emulsion (latex) paint, and 20 percent raw umber universal stainer. You should apply it with a small artist's fitch, using the illustration for guidance. The position of the larger veins is almost random. However, you will find that they look most effective if you concentrate the majority of them around and along the areas where the three glazes applied in steps 2, 3 and 4 overlap.

6 Mix a second veining glaze, consisting of 80 percent white matte emulsion (latex) paint and 20 percent yellow ochre universal stainer. Use a small artist's brush with a pointed tip to apply the glaze and create some thinner, wispier veins, and also to highlight some of the edges of the larger veins you applied in step 5. Again, size, shape and position are largely a matter of personal taste. However, you should use the illustration for guidance.

7 As you can see in this close-up view, when the glazes have dried the surface of the mantelpiece takes on a matte, slightly chalky appearance. The contrast between the darker background colours of the marble and the lighter veins is also very marked. If you are satisfied with this result, you should simply apply one or two coats of clear, matte finish emulsion (latex) glaze with a standard decorator's brush. Allow to dry for approximately 2 hours after each coat.

8 If you want to mute the colours, soften the contrast between them, and create a sheen reminiscent of polished marble, proceed as follows. Apply one or two coats of emulsion (latex) glaze with a standard decorator's brush. Alternatively, you may wish to slightly darken the finish, in which case you should mix a few drops of burnt umber universal stainer into the emulsion (latex) glaze and apply as before. In both cases, allow to dry for about 2 hours after each coat.

9 To finish off, wipe the bristles of a standard decorator's brush over some furniture wax, and brush the wax over the surface of the mantelpiece. Make sure that you get the wax into all the crevices. If you do not want to darken the colours, use a clear wax; if you do want to darken them, use a tinted (or "antiquing") wax. In both cases, let the wax set for about 30 minutes. Then buff vigorously with a lint-free cloth to produce a subtle, lustrous sheen.

Faux porphyry door

The faux porphyry finish shown here is a painted simulation of the hard, variegated, polished rock used to make architectural panelling and decorative objects such as lamp bases and candlesticks. Since the early 19th century this technique has been popular in Sweden, where it is practised as a form of spatter painting known as stenkmålning. *There are some 300 varieties of porphyry, each with subtle variations in colour and pattern; you may wish to try different colour combinations to those illustrated.*

WHAT YOU NEED

Lining paper For masking.

Sandpaper Medium-grade (grit).

White oil-based undercoat You will need about 0.5 litres (¾ UK pint/½ US quart) for an average door.

Standard decorator's brush Use a 5–7.5cm (2–3in) brush for undercoat and basecoat.

Mixing containers Use a 2.5 litre (4½ UK pint/ 2½ US quart) container for mixing the basecoat. Use three 1 litre (1¾ UK pint/ 1 US quart) containers (or old jam/glass jars) for mixing the spattering glazes.

White matte emulsion (latex) paint About one-third the quantity of undercoat.

Universal stainers Small bottles of burnt sienna and raw umber for tinting the basecoat.

Artist's oils Burnt sienna, black and white.

Transparent oil glaze About 0.5 litre (¾ UK pint/½ US quart).

White spirit (mineral spirits) Small bottle.

Flogger A soft, long-bristled brush for spattering the glazes. Buy from artist's suppliers.

Long-handled brush For tapping the flogger against (or use some wooden dowelling).

Polish Furniture polish or microcrystalline wax.

Lint-free rag For wiping spills; cleaning brushes.

1 Mask off the surrounding area with lining paper and masking tape. If the door has been previously painted, clean off any dirt or grease and key the surface (see pages 164–5) with medium-grade (grit) sandpaper. Using a medium-size standard decorator's brush, apply one or two coats of white undercoat, and allow to dry for 12 hours after each coat. If the door is bare wood you will need to seal any knots and prime it prior to undercoating (see pages 164–5).

2 Mix about 0.5 litres (¾ UK pint/½ US quart) of the porphyry basecoat, in the following proportions: 70 percent white matte emulsion (latex) paint, 20 percent burnt sienna universal stainer, and 10 percent raw umber universal stainer. Apply two coats with a standard decorator's brush, allowing a minimum of 4 hours between coats. Note: If you wish, you can substitute white eggshell for the emulsion (latex) paint and artist's oils for the universal stainers.

3 Mix the first spattering glaze as 30 percent transparent oil glaze, 20 percent white spirit (mineral spirits) and 50 percent burnt sienna artist's oil. Dip the bristle tips of a flogger brush in the glaze, and wipe off any excess on lining paper. Hold the flogger in one hand, and an old brush in the other. With the brushes about 15cm (6in) away from the door, tap the stock of the flogger against the handle of the old brush to send a fine spatter of glaze over the surface.

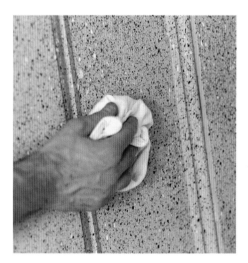

4 Recharge the flogger with glaze when necessary, and repeat step 3 until you have covered the door. Vary how hard you tap the brushes, and how far you hold them from the door, to increase and decrease the size of the spatter. Make sure that a substantial amount of basecoat still shows at this stage. Then repeat with a second glaze, consisting of 30 percent transparent oil glaze, 20 percent white spirit (mineral spirits) and 50 percent black artist's oil.

5 Mix a third glaze as follows: 30 percent transparent oil glaze, 20 percent white spirit (mineral spirits) and 50 percent white artist's oil. Apply as before, but make the coverage more random. Step back and assess the finish. You can build up any areas with any of the three glazes. You can also change to a small, square-bristled artist's brush and apply the spatter by pulling your forefinger back through the bristles. This will produce a very fine spray—ideal for filling in.

6 Allow the spatter to dry for at least 24 hours. Then, if you wish to protect the finish and create a subtle sheen across the surface that simulates polished porphyry, rub in a clear wax polish with a soft, lint-free rag. Leave the polish to harden for about 20 minutes, then buff vigorously with another clean, soft cloth. Note: There are various types of clear wax that you can use – an ordinary furniture polish will suffice, or you could use a fine microcrystalline wax if you can obtain it.

Above and left *Two unusual examples of folk graining. The log walls of a Norwegian house were decorated sometime before 1720 in the Baroque style that bears some resemblance to marquetry work; the 19th-century ladder-back chair (above) has been subtly grained to simulate a North American variety of pine.*

Folk graining

JUST AS THE TECHNIQUE OF MARBLING WAS EMPLOYED IN MANY COUNTRY HOUSES TO *represent the appearance of real marble on a range of commonplace surfaces and objects, so folk graining was used to simulate the attractive figuring, grain and patina of expensive hardwoods on plain softwood furniture and joinery. Unlike much of the graining found in urban areas, folk (or "country") graining was often a pastiche of real wood. For example, simple techniques such as dragging and combing were regularly used to suggest the figuring and grain of hardwoods, rather than produce sophisticated copies of them.*

The art of woodgraining or, as it is often referred to in country areas, folk graining, involves faking the appearance of various types and cuts of wood with paints and glazes. The earliest examples of this decorative technique date back to Egypt, thousands of years B.C. The fact that wood was rarely available to the Ancient Egyptians, and that when it could be obtained it was expensive, does much to explain why they employed artists and painters to simulate it. The subsequent development of woodgraining – right up to the present day – has always been fuelled by that same basic requirement: to suggest, as cheaply as possible, the appearance of a decorative, costly material, often in short supply. In this respect, the history of woodgraining is very similar to that of faux marbling (see pages 100–15).

In most parts of Europe, North America and Scandinavia there has never been an acute shortage of softwoods, such as the various species of pine. Fast-growing and relatively inexpensive, they have remained in plentiful supply as a construction material for joinery and furniture. However, being close-grained and displaying minimal figuring, the majority of softwoods are quite bland in appearance.

Pine graining *on the walls of a late 18th-century country mansion in Norway has been embellished with a stencilled floral frieze, and topped by a blue faux marble cornice. Also note the faux marbled cornice and plinth on the wall-hung corner cupboard.*

The figuring and grain *characteristic of pine were created on this folk-grained panelled door and architrave by dragging the bristles of a brush through a wet yellow-brown glaze, and then knocking them back with an artist's softening brush. When dry, the finish was artificially aged by brushing on a thin, translucent, gray-brown antiquing glaze.*

Fantasy folk graining *on a door, architrave, dado, and skirting (baseboard). As with the example opposite, the effect is achieved by dragging a brush through wood-coloured glaze. However, in this case the wood is of indeterminate origin, no attempt having been made to represent any particular figuring or grain.*

Glazing in detail *– this section of the door shown opposite shows how the basic antiquing glaze was augmented with a darker fine spattering glaze (used to simulate flymarks, woodworm and general discolouration).*

A simple pine doorknob *transformed by folk graining. The figuring and grain represented is characteristic of walnut. The colours are enriched, and the surface given a lustrous patina by waxing and polishing.*

On the other hand, most hardwoods can be cut to reveal intricate and often highly decorative grain and figuring. Typical examples include walnut, mahogany, oak, ash, chestnut, rosewood, satinwood and maple. Because of this, hardwoods have always been sought after for the construction of furniture, wall panelling, doors, floors, and many other items of joinery found around the home.

Unfortunately, hardwoods are slow-growing and, for the last four centuries, demand has usually outstripped supply, with costs rising accordingly. The initial response to problems of scarcity and price, particularly in the case of furniture, was to stop using thick cuts of solid hardwood and, instead, use wafer-thin cuts (veneers) glued on top of a cheaper softwood base or carcass. However, as early as the late 17th century, many high-quality veneers (notably imported Cuban mahogany and South American rosewood) also became scarce, and therefore beyond the pocket of all but the wealthiest of clients. The solution, as the Ancient Egyptians had found, was to simulate with paint.

As early as the middle of the 17th century woodgraining had gained recognition as a highly skilled art. In the cities of Europe, even many of the grandest of houses (for which the cost of real hardwoods was not a significant problem) boasted grained doors and wall-panelling. By around the middle of the 18th century, graining had become

The graining glaze *for this Shaker-style clothes press was mixed by the decorator on site, and consisted of an off-white buttermilk paint tinted with red Georgia clay. The folk-grained press is displayed in the bedroom of an 1840s plantation farmhouse in Atlanta, USA.*

A North American *19th-century dressing-table mirror. Made from a plain softwood (probably pine), it was stained to simulate mahogany. In addition, a fine-bristled brush was lightly dragged through the stain while it was still wet to suggest the close, uniform grain characteristic of the real wood.*

A combed "pine" *trunk and a folk-grained "mahogany" chest of drawers – both 19th-century – in a post-and-plank house in Texas, USA.*

A large, vinegar-grained *six-board chest stands in front of a wall-hung quilt with a "rolling star" design in a Maine farmhouse, USA.*

A late 18th-century *Swedish wall-hung cupboard. Made of pine, it was folk-grained with a deep brown glaze to simulate stained oak.*

A 19th-century *domed-top, combed trunk stands at the foot of a bed in a farmhouse in Texas, USA. The quilt features the "seven stars" pattern.*

Folk graining *was much in evidence in Scandinavian country houses from the 17th to the 19th century. This magnificent, folk-grained, Norwegian bureau-bookcase is from the same house and period as the armoire shown on pages 124–5. The contrasting white and gray door, lid and drawer panels reflect the influence of Swedish-style decoration at this time.*

sufficiently fashionable to also appear in many less-affluent urban households. A fully panelled, hardwood-grained room was considered a symbol of wealth and status (even though it cost substantially less than the real thing).

From the late 18th to the mid-19th century, increasingly accurate painted facsimiles of woods were produced in the urban houses of Europe and North America. This was largely a result of artists and painters improving their graining techniques by reading a number of specialist books published on the subject. As with faux marble finishes (see pages 100–15), one of the chief exponents of the art was an Englishman, Thomas Kershaw, much of whose work, even under the closest scrutiny, was indistinguishable from real wood.

The highly sophisticated replications of hardwoods available to many urban householders during the 19th century did not, however, fuel an ever-greater demand for this decorative technique. Indeed, apart from a brief spell during the 1880s, when it became fashionable to grain the walls of libraries, dining rooms and hallways in oak, walnut, mahogany, chestnut, and even softwood pine, mass-produced wallpaper supplanted woodgraining as a wall finish, particularly in drawing rooms and salons. However, high quality hardwood graining did remain a desirable finish on softwood furniture, and on architectural fixtures and fittings such as stair, dado and picture rails, and doors, architraves and skirtings (baseboards).

With the exception of a few grander country houses, the woodgraining found in the rural areas of Europe, North America and Scandinavia was far less sophisticated than its urban counterpart, even during the 19th century. The desire to decorate softwood furniture and joinery with exotic and prestigious hard-wood finishes was no less great than in urban areas. However, the itinerant crafts-men and homeowners who practised woodgraining in provincial areas had far less access to useful reference material (both imported exotic hardwoods and technical publications on the subject) than the specialist painters who worked in the cities. Moreover, the mediums and equipment rural artists and painters used to simulate figuring and grain were often cruder (and certainly cheaper) than the more refined paints, glazes and specialist graining tools available in urban areas.

Some of the best examples of this cruder, rustic folk graining are to be found on joinery and furniture in rural North American and Scandi-navian homes dating from the mid-17th to the end of the 19th century. Instead of using transparent oil glazes tinted with refined artist's oil paints

Sophisticated and exuberant *folk graining, dating from c.1801, on a large armoire and a door in a Norwegian country house. The simulated crown or flame figuring is most commonly found on sawn timbers of oak, elm, chestnut and ash.*

(as in the cities), the itinerant craftsmen of country areas invariably employed simple earth-coloured pigments mixed with locally available mediums, such as vinegar, beer and distemper. Also, instead of using specialist graining brushes, such as mottlers (spalters) and badger softeners, to manipulate the glaze and simulate the grain and figuring of the wood, they relied on materials and objects as diverse as pieces of cork, combs cut from leather or oiled card, and leaves from various species of plant. They even used their fingers. The results often bore only a passing resemblance to the natural colours, the figuring and the grain, and the subtle, lustrous patina of waxed and polished hardwoods. This is certainly the case with the "fantasy" black-on-dull-red graining found in numerous Swedish and Norwegian country houses and farms. It also applies to the many examples of colourful dragged joinery and combed furniture in rural North American homes.

It follows that most rustic folk graining, unlike much urban woodgraining, rarely deceives anyone into believing that he or she is looking at real hardwood. However, folk graining often has a stylized, theatrical quality that simply suggests the appearance of wood. In that sense, there is no deliberate deception taking place. Instead, the onlooker is simply being invited to knowingly admire the painted illusion for what it is, rather than what it pretends to be.

Oak-grained cupboard

The woodgraining finish here is a simulation of oak. If you look at various pieces of furniture made from real oak you will notice marked differences in the pattern of the grain and, especially, the figuring of the wood. This is a result of the way in which the wood has been cut, and these differences have been reflected here: the door panel shows oak heart grain, while the sides show quartered oak flares. However, there is no reason why you should not swop their positions, or use just one of them on both the door and sides.

WHAT YOU NEED

Dust sheet For protecting the floor.

Primer/undercoat About 0.5 litres (1 UK pint/ ½ US quart) of a white oil-based type.

Standard decorator's brushes Sizes 2.5, 5, and 7.5cm (1, 2, and 3in).

Dull-yellow eggshell paint About the same quantity as for the primer/undercoat.

Mixing containers Four or five, each with a capacity of 1 litre (1¾ UK pints/1 US quart).

Transparent oil (scumble) glaze You will need less than 0.5 litres (1 UK pint/½ US quart).

Artist's oils Small tubes of burnt umber and black, for the graining glazes.

White spirit (mineral spirits) You will need a small bottle.

Artist's flogger A large, long-bristled flogging brush for basic graining and softening.

Artist's brushes Buy one pointed tip and one flat fitch (hog's hair) both 5mm (¼in).

Lint-free rag Mopping spills; cleaning brushes.

Combing tool Made from card or plastic. Available from artist's suppliers and craft stores.

Button polish (shellac) A refined type of French polish.

Wire (steel) wool Fine-grade 0000, for applying wax polish.

Furniture polish Use tinted or clear furniture wax for polishing the finish.

1 Begin by preparing the bare or already painted wood (as described on pages 164–9). Next, using a standard decorator's brush, apply a minimum of two coats of an oil-based, white primer/undercoat, to obliterate the underlying wood or paint. Allow at least 8 hours' drying time after each coat. Then brush on two coats of a dull-yellow eggshell paint. This time, allow a minimum of 12 hours' drying time after each coat.

2 Mix up the basic graining glaze: 50 percent transparent oil glaze, 20 percent burnt umber artist's oil, 10 percent black artist's oil, and 20 percent white spirit (mineral spirits). Decide which part of the cupboard you wish to start on – in this case the door – as you must complete steps 2 and 3 before the glaze dries. Then, use a standard decorator's brush to apply one reasonably even coat of the graining glaze.

3 To establish the background grain of oak, hold the bristles of an artist's flogger brush parallel to the surface of the door. Lightly tap the sides of the bristles up and down the surface in a series of slightly overlapping, vertical and parallel bands. This removes tiny specks of glaze and creates irregular-shaped pores over the surface. Keep cleaning the bristles on a lint-free rag. Repeat steps 2 and 3 on the rest of the cupboard.

4 Leave the first glaze to dry for 24 hours. Mix a second graining glaze consisting of 40 percent transparent oil glaze, 20 percent white spirit (mineral spirits), 25 percent burnt umber artist's oil, and 15 percent black artist's oil. Brush a thin coat of transparent oil glaze over the the door. When it becomes tacky (after about 15 minutes), apply the heart grain using the second graining glaze and a flat fitch. Use the illustration to help establish the pattern of the grain.

5 With some sections of the heart grain it is more effective to use a combing tool (made from either card or plastic). This is best done where the figuring takes the form a series of gently undulating, parallel and vertical lines. To reproduce this, first apply the glaze with the artist's brush, as before. Then, hold the comb vertically and drag it from top to bottom down through the wet glaze. At the end of each run, wipe off any excess glaze from the teeth onto a clean lint-free rag.

6 Once you have completed the heart grain, you can leave it as it is if you are trying to create a slightly cruder or coarser finish. However, if want to produce a softer, more subtle finish (as was done here), dab the glaze with an artist's flogger brush. The basic technique required is the same as the one you employed in step 3. However, this time you must wait until the glaze is tacky before starting, and then use an even lighter dabbing action with the bristles.

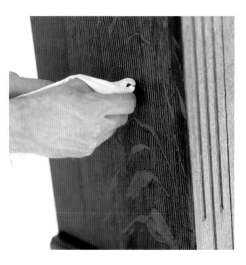

7 Move onto one of the sides of the cupboard, which should have already had its basic grain applied using the technique shown and described in steps 2 and 3. Return to the first graining glaze that you applied in step 2, and brush one coat of it over the surface with a standard decorator's brush. A meticulous application is not required at this stage, although it will help the next stage if you make sure that you finish off your brush strokes in a vertical direction.

8 The next stage in the build-up of the quarter-cut oak flares requires you to pull the teeth of a combing tool through the still-wet glaze. This time, hold the comb horizontally, and pull it lightly down from top to bottom in a series of slightly overlapping parallel bands. At the end of each sweep, wipe off the build-up of glaze in the teeth onto a clean lint-free rag. If you find that the glaze is drying too quickly, simply brush on some more and repeat the combing action.

9 To create the flares take a piece of clean, lint-free rag and wrap it around the end of one of your forefingers. Lightly wipe it through the still-wet glaze, in a series of irregular-shaped and irregular-spaced arcs. Complete each flare in one sweep, and then reposition the rag around your finger so that you start each flare with a clean surface. The spacing of the flares is a matter of composition, but use the illustration (or a piece of real quarter-cut oak) for reference.

10 Once again, you have a choice at this point. If you want to produce a cruder, coarser finish, you can leave the flares as they are. However, if you want a softer, more subtle finish (as was done here), lightly dab up and down over the tacky glaze with the sides of the bristles of an artist's flogger (as in step 6). Remember to keep wiping off the build-up of glaze on the bristles onto a piece of clean, lint-free rag.

11 Having completed the other side of the cupboard, leave the glaze to dry for a minimum of 24 hours. To protect the finish, and to give it a glossy sheen, apply one coat of neat button polish (shellac), using a standard decorator's brush. Do not overbrush, or you may leave unsightly brushmarks on the surface, and try to finish off your brushstrokes in the direction of the grain. Then leave to dry for about 6 hours.

12 To cut back the shine of the button polish (shellac), and to produce a subtle, lustrous patina, wipe a piece of fine grade wire (steel) wool over some furniture wax, and gently rub it back and forth over the finish (always in the direction of the grain). You can use a clear wax if you are happy with the colour of the oak, or a tinted one if you wish to slightly darken it. Finally, buff to a sheen with a soft, lint-free rag.

Combed trunk

Combing was a popular method of decorating furniture in the rural areas of North America and Scandinavia during the 18th and 19th centuries. A relatively simple technique, it involves dragging the teeth of a comb (which is traditionally cut from cardboard, bone or metal) through a wet glaze to produce parallel wavy lines offset by a contrasting coloured basecoat. In essence it is a very crude type of woodgraining: the lines and colours being a pastiche, rather than a replication, of the figuring and grain of real wood.

WHAT YOU NEED

Wooden or metal spatula To remove leather.

Wire (steel) wool Buy grade 3 and grade 0000.

Plaster filler (spackle) To provide a level surface for combing.

Standard decorator's brushes You will need two – sizes 2.5cm (1in) and 5cm (2in).

White primer/undercoat For an unpainted trunk you will need about 1 litre (1¾ UK pint/1 US quart).

Fawn/mustard eggshell paint You will need about 0.5 litre (1 UK pint/½ US quart) for the basecoat.

Sandpaper Medium and fine grades (grits).

Transparent oil (scumble) glaze Small tin.

White spirit (mineral spirits) Small bottle.

Artist's intenso colours Raw and burnt umber.

Small mixing containers Three or four.

Artist's palette For mixing the paints.

Combing tool Purchase 2.5cm (1in) and 5cm (2in) plastic or cardboard combs.

Lint-free rag For cleaning comb.

Button polish (shellac) Small bottle.

Clear furniture wax Small tin.

Black metal paint With a built-in corrosion converter and stabilizer (see pages 164–9).

1 Traditionally, combing was most often applied to storage boxes such as trunks. It is particularly effective on domed-top versions. Examples dating from the 18th and 19th centuries are quite rare (and costly) nowadays. However, early 20th-century travelling trunks bound in poor quality leather are reasonably plentiful, and inexpensive. The old leather can be easily removed by dampening with hot water and scraping off with a steel wallpaper spatula.

2 Rub down any iron retaining bands with grade 3 wire (steel) wool to key the surface and remove any rust. Mix up some plaster filler (spackle) to the consistency of very thick cream and spread it over the wood with a metal spatula or a standard decorator's brush. Build it up in layers, and when dry rub with sandpaper, to produce a smooth surface. Apply a white primer/undercoat and, when dry, brush on two coats of fawn or mustard eggshell paint.

3 Allow the eggshell basecoats to dry for at least 24 hours. Next, mix the combing glaze as: 40 percent transparent oil glaze, 20 percent white spirit (mineral spirits), 20 percent raw umber intenso colour, and 20 percent burnt umber intenso colour. Apply the glaze quite thickly with a standard decorator's brush over two or three of the wooden panels. Do not cover more than this at any one time as the glaze must be wet or, at the very least, still tacky for the combing.

4 Grip a combing tool between your thumb and fingers. Starting at one end of the panel, drag the comb through the wet glaze in a continuous wave-shaped sweep to the other end. Clean the teeth of the comb with lint-free rag, and repeat in a series of parallel sweeps to finish the panel. Work quickly, or the glaze may dry before you can comb it. If it does dry, wipe it down with a rag moistened with white spirit (mineral spirits) and apply more glaze as in step 3.

5 When all the panels are completed, leave the trunk to dry for at least 24 hours. Working quickly (and avoiding any overbrushing that might leave marks in the finish), brush a coat of button polish (shellac) over the panels. The button polish (shellac) will seal the combing glaze and give the finish a high-gloss sheen. You can lessen the sheen when dry by gently rubbing on clear furniture wax with fine grade 000 wire (steel) wool, and then buffing with a soft cloth.

6 To finish, you will need to paint any iron bands and locks. The best way of doing this is to carefully brush on a commercial black metal paint containing a rust converter and stabilizer. These paints provide very good coverage, so usually only one coat will be necessary. However, they also give off unpleasant fumes that can be harmful if inhaled for any length of time. So, work in a well-ventilated area, wear a face mask, and keep children and animals well away.

Vinegar-grained mirror

Vinegar graining is a fairly simple technique, and has been much used in previous centuries, notably in North America, to simulate the figuring and grain of exotic (and expensive) hardwoods on plain softwoods. It is particularly suited to the reproduction of bird's eye maple, as shown here. It is a good idea to try to obtain a piece of real bird's eye maple to use as reference. However, you should remember that with rustic graining the aim is to represent the appearance of the wood (or produce a pastiche of it), rather than meticulously replicate it.

WHAT YOU NEED

Masking tape For protecting mirror glass.

White primer/undercoat Less than 300ml (½ UK pint/⅓ US quart) of an oil-based type.

Standard decorator's brushes You will need three 2.5cm (1in) brushes.

Yellow milk paint Less than 300ml (½ UK pint/⅓ US quart).

White matte emulsion (latex) paint About 75ml (⅛ UK pint/2 US cups).

Fuller's earth A tablespoonful.

Lint-free rag For wiping the frame.

Artist's powder pigments Teaspoonfuls of burnt sienna, raw sienna and raw umber.

White vinegar 150ml (¼ UK pint/1 US cup).

Artist's palette For mixing glaze.

Mixing containers Two 1 litre (1¾ UK pint/ 1 US quart) plastic or metal containers.

Small artist's mottler (spalter) For producing figuring and graining in the glaze.

Artist's softening brush Badger or hog's hair.

Button polish (shellac)

Wire (steel) wool Fine grade 000.

Beeswax furniture polish Clear or tinted.

White spirit (mineral spirits) Use this to clean brushes.

1 Having masked off the mirror glass, brush on two coats of a white, oil-based primer/undercoat to the pine frame. Allow to dry for at least 12 hours after each coat. Next, brush on one or two basecoats, consisting of 70 percent yellow milk paint and 30 percent white matte emulsion (latex) paint. Leave each coat to dry thoroughly for about 12 hours. Then wipe a small quantity of Fuller's earth over the surface of the frame with a clean, lint-free cotton rag.

2 Make up a vinegar glaze consisting of approximately 10 percent burnt sienna artist's powder pigment, 20 percent raw sienna powder pigment, 10 percent raw umber powder pigment, and 60 percent white vinegar. In total, you will only need about 150ml (¼ UK pint/½ US cup) of glaze to cover an average-size frame. Using a standard decorator's brush, apply one coat of the glaze over one side of the frame. Cover it as evenly as possible, and try to avoid overbrushing it.

3 Working reasonably quickly – before the glaze starts to become tacky – drag a small artist's mottler (spalter) through the glaze. Start at one end of the side and drag in a continuous sweep to the other end, introducing a subtle undulating movement as you work your way along. The slightly wavy lines left in the glaze simulate the basic figuring and grain of bird's eye maple. At the end of each drag, clean the bristles on a rag.

4 Decant a little white vinegar into a small container. Dip your forefinger into it and then lightly touch the still-wet glaze. The vinegar causes a localized reaction, which disperses the glazes outward from the point of contact. The result is similar in appearance to the small, circular knots (bird's eyes) that are the distinguishing feature of the maple. As well as the illustrations, refer to a real piece of maple to help with the position and spacing of the knots (bird's eyes).

5 While the glaze is slightly tacky, lightly brush over the surface in all directions with an artist's softening brush. The aim is to reduce any hard edges in the glaze around the knots (bird's eyes) or figuring and grain, and thereby soften the appearance of the finish. A fine-bristled badger softener is the best tool for this. However, it is expensive, and a coarser hog's hair softener is an acceptable alternative. Then repeat steps 2–5 on the other sides of the frame.

6 Brush on one coat of button polish (shellac), and allow to dry for about 8 hours. Then dab a small piece of fine grade 000 wire (steel) wool into some clear (or slightly tinted) furniture polish. Gently rub the wool and polish back and forth over the frame in the direction of the grain. Renew the polish as necessary. The wire (steel) wool will reduce the high sheen of the button polish (shellac). Finally, buff the polish with a soft, lint-free cloth to produce a smooth, satin finish.

Above and left *Whether they have been carved, sawn or turned, wooden utensils, joinery and furniture often play an important aesthetic and functional role in the everyday life of country homes. Their natural beauty can be enhanced by the application of a wide range of traditional stains, oils, polishes and waxes.*

Liming & staining

WHILE COLOURWASHING, PAINTING, STENCILLING, MARBLING AND FOLK GRAINING WERE the favoured means of decorating furniture and joinery made from softwoods, they were invariably discarded in favour of staining, waxing and liming where hardwoods were concerned. The reason for this was that, unlike the majority of softwoods, most hardwoods (notably oak and mahogany) display attractive figuring and grain – features obscured by painted decoration. Thus, liming mixtures were used to highlight the grain, while stains and waxes enhanced both figuring and grain, and enriched the colour of the natural wood.

In the rural areas of North America, Scandinavia and Europe a wide range of media have been employed over the last five centuries to enhance the natural beauty of wood. The most notable and enduring of these have been liming pastes and waxes, stains and dyes, oils, wax polishes and varnishes.

Liming pastes and waxes were used to lighten or bleach the natural colour of wood, and also provide a degree of protection against insect infestation. Traditionally they were applied to furniture, wall-panelling, floors and other items of joinery made from open-grained hardwoods such as oak and ash, although they have also been used on close-grained softwoods such as pine. Despite being most commonly associated with Scandinavian interiors of the 18th and 19th centuries, liming pastes and waxes were also used in European country houses during the 16th century, and in rustic North American homes from the Colonial period to the end of the 19th century.

Liming waxes are best suited to open-grained woods, while liming pastes are more appropriate for closer-grained wood and exposed surfaces (such as floors) that are subject to considerable wear and tear (and thus also require varnishing). Today, pre-mixed commercial pastes and waxes are available from specialist decorating retailers. You can also prepare them yourself – see pages 146–7 for information on how to mix and apply a traditional liming paste.

Designer Christophe Decarpentrie *imported this pair of studded and limewashed Moroccan doors to hang at the entrance of the sleeping quarters in his home in Brussels, Belgium. Aside from its aesthetic properties, the limewash helps to protect the wood from insect infestation – a preventative measure very necessary in North Africa.*

The principal living area *in The Malt House, a residential conversion on the outskirts of Bath in Somerset, England. The bare pine floorboards were treated with a thin liming mixture. The modern beech table, designed by Richard Latrobe Bateman, is unstained. The tabletop was given a protective, clear wax finish.*

A mahogany-stained, *Canadian "shoefoot" cupboard, used to store a collection of patchwork quilts in a farmhouse in Maine, USA.*

This English mahogany settle *was stripped back to the bare wood by its current owner, and then painted with a white wood stain. Although this was not intended, the stain reacted with the wood to produce a ghostly blue tone across the surface of the piece that is reminiscent of liming.*

A weathered pine *bench on a porch at Seaside in Florida, USA. Linseed oil can be rubbed into the wood to prevent it drying out and splitting.*

A particularly fine example of *an early 18th-century stained, waxed and polished settle. Pieces made in this style are often referred to as "bacon settles", because the tall cupboard set into the back provided a space for hanging a side of bacon. There is also a storage box underneath the seat.*

Two fine antique chairs *in a room at Frog Pool Farm, in Avon, England. Both chairs are stained and polished walnut. The chair that stands to the left of the door was made during the reign of James II (1685–88), while the chair to the right is mid-17th-century, from Lancashire, England.*

A 19th-century, French *provincial armoire, with crisply carved decorations on the door panels. Stained and regularly polished, it has developed a soft, lustrous patina across its surface, and now stands in the bedroom of a country house in Connecticut, USA.*

This 19th-century, wax-polished *pine cupboard was originally the lower half of a dresser. Numerous pieces were made in this style during the 18th and 19th centuries, and while some were originally painted, just as many were simply waxed or oiled to bring out the natural grain and figuring of the wood.*

A large custom-made *built-in pine dresser. In urban houses, during the 18th, 19th and 20th centuries, pieces such as this were often painted. However, in country areas the quietly understated figuring and grain and the warm mellow tones of this abundant softwood were shown the light of day.*

To mix a traditional liming wax, place a mixing bowl in a saucepan of water. Put a block of pure beeswax into the bowl. Gently heat the water in the saucepan until the wax melts, making sure that none of the water boils over into the bowl. Mix titanium white powder pigment into the wax (in a ratio of one part powder to three parts wax). Pour off the mixture into a separate container, and leave it to set. Rub it into the surface of the wood with a cotton rag. Leave for about 30 minutes, then rub off excess wax with a clean rag and buff to a subtle sheen.

To enhance, adjust, or radically change the natural colour of wood, four basic types of wood stain are used: water-based, oil-based, spirit-based, and chemical-based. Water-based stains (also known as direct dyes) are made by dissolving earth-coloured powder pigments in water, and are most success-fully applied to light-coloured, close-grained woods, such as beech and pine. However, porous softwoods absorb them unevenly, which can result in patchy colouration. Water-based stains can also raise the grain of the wood, which then requires sanding down and sealing with shellac prior to waxing and polishing.

The majority of oil-based stains are a mixture of oil pigments, white spirit (mineral spirits) and naphtha (a liquid distillation from coal tar). Unlike water-based stains, they do not raise the grain, and they provide a more even colouration. However, they are slow to dry, quite expensive and tended to be restricted to better-quality pieces of hardwood furniture.

Spirit-based wood stains are made by dissolving powder pigments in methylated spirits (denatured alcohol), and adding shellac in a ratio of one part shellac to four parts spirits. They produce duller colours than water-based stains, and tend to be used on oily, hard and fine-grained woods. Like water-based stains, they raise the grain and, as they dry quickly, are difficult to apply evenly over large areas.

Chemical stains are made by dissolving chemicals such as copper sulphate, biochromate of potash, blue copperas and ammonia in water. In skilled hands they produce remarkably subtle results. For example, ammonia turns mahogany a deep brown colour with a slightly grayish cast, blue copperas gives most species of wood a light gray hue, and biochromate of potash turns beech a light tan and walnut pale yellow. All of them work by reacting with the tannic acid in the wood. However, it is difficult to predict how much tannic acid is present, and therefore hard to control the final colouration.

Having made adjustments to the natural colour of the wood (which, of course, isn't always necessary), there are various options available for the finish. As far as country furniture was concerned this means an oil or a wax polish. Oil finishes are usually restricted to open-grained woods, such as oak, teak and

An early 19th-century *stick-back chair stands next to a varnished pine storage cupboard, and below an unusual painted pine wall cupboard. While relatively inexpensive softwoods such as pine were either painted or unpainted in country houses, furniture made from more costly hardwoods, such as this oak chair, was invariably stained and oiled or waxed.*

An eclectic assortment of *18th-, 19th- and early 20th-century country furniture lies at the heart of this kitchen, giving it an instantly recognisable "country style". Apart from the slightly distressed, green-painted storage cupboard, all the pieces boast the warm tones and subtle figuring and grains of the woods from which they are made.*

A naturally weathered, *five-plank pine bench. Intended for use out-of-doors, it is seasonally varnished to protect against moisture.*

The branches and twigs *that make up this rustic American porch chair would have been whittled to shape, and oiled or varnished for protection.*

A North American *rustic ladderback rocking chair. It was intended for use outside (on a porch), and has been allowed to weather naturally.*

A natural oak stable *door, with iron hinges and latches, in designer Stephen Mack's 18th-century, North-American country home.*

Turned on a lathe, *bowls such as this were produced throughout the rural communities of Europe, North America and Scandinavia. They are mostly used in kitchens for storing and mixing foodstuffs, but here the bowl serves as a soap dish. To protect against moisture, the natural resins in the wood can be augmented with a light application of vegetable oil.*

A 19th-century carved wooden *butter mould depicting (appropriately enough) a dairy cow. All manner of functional and decorative treen wares, such as this, were produced in rural communities where timber was in plentiful supply. They were often carved and whittled in front of the fire during the long cold winter months.*

Wooden cutting boards *are found in urban and rural kitchens alike. However, this pair of pig-shaped boards can be immediately located to the country. Untreated sycamore, beech or maple provide the desired combination of close-graining, absence of intrinsic taste and smell, stability and resistance to moisture required for a durable cutting board.*

hardwoods imported from Central America. Raw linseed oil was sometimes used. However, because of its very slow drying time (up to three days), boiled linseed oil was usually preferred, as it dried within 24 hours. Nowadays, commercial teak oil is also a favoured alternative. In each case, the method of application is as follows: Pour a generous quantity of oil onto a cotton rag, and rub it into the surface of the wood. Leave for two or three minutes, then wipe off the excess with a clean rag. Apply one or two more coats, allowing eight hours' drying time for teak oil, 24 hours for boiled linseed oil, and 72 hours for raw linseed oil, between each coat. Then buff to a sheen with a soft cloth.

Traditional wax polishes came in a number of formulations. For example, a hard, durable wax suitable for solid wooden furniture was made by melting pure beeswax and carnuba wax together, and then mixing them with turpentine or denatured alcohol in a ratio of 1:3. Once re-set, they formed a hard polish that is brushed or scrubbed into the wood, left for two or three hours, and then buffed to a deep lustrous sheen with a soft rag. A slightly softer and less durable alternative was produced the same way, but without the carnuba wax. Also, a cotton rag, rather than a brush, was used to apply the polish. Variations on both types were made by adding earth-coloured pigments to darken the finish. In most cases, however, a thin coat of shellac (or button polish) was brushed onto the wood and allowed to dry before the wax was applied. The purpose of the shellac was to seal the surface and stop the wax penetrating the wood and, because it absorbs dirt, turning the wood slightly gray.

Occasionally, various types of clear or slightly tinted varnish would be used to provide a finish on lesser pieces of country furniture. However, for the most part, varnishes were used on joinery, such as wall-panelling, doors, stair rails and risers, skirting (base boards) and exterior wall cladding. Traditional country varnishes can be divided into two basic types: spirit-based and oil-based.

The clear spirit varnish used on interior joinery was made by mixing one pound of shellac resin with one-sixth of a gallon of denatured alcohol, and leaving it to stand for 24 hours before straining out any impurities. One or more coats were then brushed over the wood and allowed to dry to a mid-glossy sheen. Slightly tinted versions were made by adding lac (a resin) to the mixture, which gave the wood an orange-red colour cast. A typical oil-based varnish for interior use was prepared by slowly heating linseed oil to thicken it, and then brushing it on. For exteriors, or where damp was a problem, an oil-based varnish consisting of drying oil and litharge proved effective. However, during the latter part of the 20th century, commercial polyurethane varnishes have tended to supersede these early concoctions.

The standard of craftsmanship *that went into the making of wooden artefacts in country areas was often very high. The method of construction – the decorative carving and the general attention to detail – on this charming, shellacked and waxed, late 18th-century spice box is equivalent to that found on many better quality pieces of furniture of the period.*

A traditional, wall-hung, *stained pine knife and spoon rack. All shapes and sizes, the spoons are 19th-century and carved from sycamore.*

An early 20th-century *egg storage box. Unlike the spice box shown opposite, which displays many of the qualities of the cabinet-maker's art, this box is of relatively crude construction. The carcass is made from butt-jointed stained pine, and features nailed tin corner brackets and an iron latch, carrying handle and hinges. The padlock is brass.*

A 19th-century *painted pine spoon rack. Occasionally the spoons can be treated with vegetable oil to prevent splitting and cracking.*

Even after the *adoption of metal cutlery in country households during the 20th century, wooden handles often remained the preferred option.*

Wooden handles *need to be stained and waxed in order to make sure that the wood is not damaged by washing water.*

Two wooden rolling *pins, turned on a simple, manually operated lathe, and a butter pat – all of 19th-century North-American origin.*

An 18th-century *carved knife and spoon. In many country areas, forks only came into general use during the latter part of the 19th century.*

Limed floorboards

The liming technique shown here is a traditional means of decorating wood, particularly in England and Scandinavia. It is demonstrated on bare floorboards, but can be applied equally successfully to other joinery, such as wall-panelling. It looks most effective on oak or pine. Both of these have a reasonably open grain (unlike, for example, walnut) into which the liming glaze can accumulate. The opacity of the glaze in the grain then contrasts tonally with the thinner, more translucent coating it provides on the rest of the wooden surface.

WHAT YOU NEED

Hammer and nail punch (setter) For knocking/pounding down floorboard nails.

Floor sander (optional.) Can be rented from a hire company, together with coarse and medium grades (grits) of sandpaper.

Large plastic bucket For soaking the animal glue granules.

Wooden stick For stirring the animal hide glue.

Animal hide glue Also known as rabbit-skin glue. For the floorboards of an average-size room you will need approximately 0.5kg (1lb) in granule form.

Old saucepan Medium size.

Small camping stove For warming the liming glaze on site.

Mixing bowl Ceramic or heat-proof glass. Should be of a size that fits inside the saucepan, resting on its rim, without touching the bottom.

Large spoons Two for mixing the glaze.

Whiting (powdered chalk/limestone) You will need about 0.125kg (4oz).

Standard decorator's brush Two 10–15cm (4–6in) brushes.

Matte acrylic emulsion (latex) glaze You will need about 0.5 litre (1 UK pint/½ US quart).

1 Secure any loose floorboards and, using a hammer and nail punch (setter), knock all nail heads just below the surface of the boards. If the boards are new, proceed to step 2. If they are old and are stained, painted, varnished or dirty they must be sanded down. Do this with a rented industrial sander, working your way diagonally across the boards, following the accompanying manufacturer's instructions. Use a coarse-grade (grit) sandpaper first. Finish off with a medium-grade (grit).

2 Fill a large plastic bucket with approximately 3 litres (6 UK pints/2¾ US quarts) of cold water. Using a long wooden stick, gradually stir in about 0.5kg (1lb) of animal hide (rabbit-skin) glue granules, and leave to soak overnight. By the following morning the granules will have absorbed the water and expanded dramatically (this is why you need a large bucket). At this stage the mixture will have attained the consistency of a lumpy cake mix. Stir once again to get rid of any lumps.

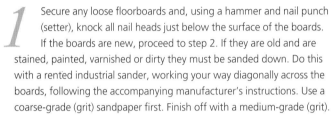

3 Pour 1 litre (1¾ UK pints/1 US quart) of water into a medium-size saucepan and bring to a boil on a stove. Turn down the heat and allow the water to gently simmer. Spoon the glue into a heatproof mixing bowl, and place the bowl in the saucepan (with the top of the bowl resting on the rim of the saucepan). Do not allow any water to mix with the glue. During the next hour the glue will gradually melt. Do not stir the mixture or allow it to boil. Once the glue has melted, spoon off any impurities from the surface, and slowly mix in 125kg (4oz) of whiting.

4 Keeping the liming mixture warm on the stove, apply one coat to the surface of the floorboards with a large standard decorator's brush. Allow to dry for about 8 hours. The glaze will become increasing opaque, white and chalky-looking. You may then wish to apply a second coat (gently re-heat the glaze, if necessary). Once the glaze has dried, brush on a protective coat of matte acrylic emulsion (latex) glaze. Initially this will make the liming glaze more translucent, but in about 2 hours it will dry back to its original opacity and chalkiness.

Stained & polished chair

The staining, waxing and polishing technique shown here is a reasonably quick and easy means of reviving broken-down finishes on older pieces of furniture, and of quickly antiquing newer items. Part of the "ageing" process involves staining and darkening the wood. The extent to which you do this is a matter of choice, and can be adjusted by altering the proportion of pigment added to the polish. However, if you think the piece you wish to treat may be rare or valuable, seek professional advice first as you could devalue it.

WHAT YOU NEED

Lint-free rag For removing any grease marks.

Old towelling (terrycloth) Use with soapy water to remove any dirt.

White spirit (mineral spirits) A small bottle for removing the old finish.

Methylated spirits (denatured alcohol) See white spirit (mineral spirits) above.

Wire (steel) wool You will need fine grades 00 and 0000.

Varnish stripper If you need to use this to remove the old finish you must work in a well-ventilated area and wear rubber (household) gloves to protect your hands from the caustic fluid.

Artist's palette Use to blend powder pigments.

Small mixing containers Three or four old glass (jam) jars will suffice.

Button polish (shellac)

Artist's powder pigments Small quantities of burnt umber and raw umber.

Standard decorator's brush Two 5cm (2in) versions are the most useful size.

Cotton wool (swabs) For the "rubbing" pad.

Tinted furniture wax Buy a hard-paste version, rather than a cream or spray.

1. Begin by assessing the condition of the chair (noting the warning about valuable antiques mentioned in the introduction opposite). If the original finish is dirty, but basically sound, before proceeding to step 3 simply wash down the chair with lukewarm soapy water and a lint-free rag. Next, rinse with clean water; dry thoroughly with old towelling (terrycloth). Any grease marks can be removed with a rag moistened with white spirit (mineral spirits). If, however, the chair has been button polished or varnished, and this has begun to flake off, you will need to take slightly more drastic action. Wash, rinse and dry as above, then proceed to step 2.

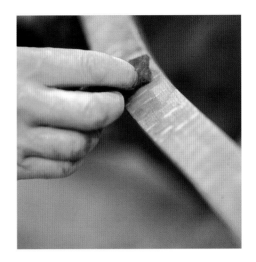

2. In this example the old button polish (shellac) was flaking in places. Remove this by gently rubbing back and forth along the grain of the wood with methylated spirits (denatured alcohol) and grade 00 wire (steel) wool. Work on a section at a time, wiping off the liquefied polish with lint-free rag. If your chair has been varnished, wear rubber gloves and use a commercial varnish stripper. Then lightly rub over the chair with a rag moistened with white spirit (mineral spirits).

3. Using the artist's palette and small mixing containers, make up a glaze consisting of 70 percent button polish (shellac), 20 percent burnt umber powder pigment, and 10 percent raw umber powder pigment. To darken the glaze add more burnt umber; to lighten it use less burnt umber. Apply the glaze with a brush to one section of the chair at a time. Work quickly, but do not overbrush or you may leave marks in the finish. Then leave to dry for at least 4 hours.

4. Make a "rubbing" pad by wrapping some lint-free rag around a half-handful of cotton wool. Pour some button polish (shellac) into the cotton wool and tighten the rag around it, gathering the folds in your hand and ensuring the face of the pad is crease-free. When the polish soaks through to the face, rub it over a section of the chair. Work in a figure-eight movement, keeping the pad in constant contact with the surface until you have finished the section.

5. Repeat step 4 on the other sections of the chair and allow the polish to dry for at least 4 hours. If you wish, you can then apply further coats of button polish (shellac): the more you apply, the deeper the shine. Once the final coat has dried, wipe a piece of fine grade 0000 wire (steel) wool over some tinted furniture wax and lightly rub it back and forth over the surface (in the direction of the grain). Leave for an hour, then buff to a soft, lustrous sheen with a soft lint-free rag.

Above and left *The contrasting colours and textures of metal and ceramic artefacts, fixtures and fittings found in the typical country home are vividly illustrated by a 19th-century copper bath tub in the bathroom of a French manoir, and a locally made terra cotta pot and a Moroccan lantern in a house on Gran Canaria, in Spain.*

Ceramics & metal

CERAMICS AND METALWARES HAVE ALWAYS PLAYED A CRUCIAL ROLE IN THE FUNCTIONING *and in the aesthetics of country homes. Invariably both useful and decorative, they include items as diverse as stoneware and earthenware storage vessels, punched-tin cabinets, wrought-iron fenders, copper flatware, and brass and bronze candlesticks. Their attractiveness lies not only in the original colours and textures of the materials from which they are made, but also in the patina that gradually accumulates over their surfaces as a result of general wear-and-tear, and exposure to light, heat, moisture and air.*

The non-precious metals most commonly found in traditional country homes in Europe, Scandinavia and North America were iron, tin, copper, brass, and pewter. The objects made from these metals were invariably functional, but they were also usually decorative as well.

Copper, brass and pewter wares are prime examples of this. Pans, plates, bowls, jugs, mugs and ladles are just a few of the items from the *batterie de cuisine* of a rural kitchen. For ease of access they were usually placed on open shelves, or hung from hooks on the walls or ceiling. Such an arrangement was not only practical: gleaming rows of polished metalwares introduced attractive shapes and colours that made the kitchen a more enjoyable place to work and eat in. They were also a statement of wealth.

Tin was also a much-used metal in rural areas. Made in sheet form, it is easily cut into decorative shapes. Thus, objects as diverse as candle-holders, colanders, biscuit moulds, pastry cutters, cheese graters and baking tins were all produced from this cheap, versatile alloy. The thinness of tin also made it suitable for punching: a handicraft that involves striking a nail punch through a tin surface to create a series of holes that make up a pattern or motif (see pages 156–7). Typical motifs included stars, hearts, flowers and leaves, and these often appear on punched-tin panels inserted into wooden cupboards (meat or pie safes).

This French milk jug *dating from the late 19th-century was bought for a few francs at a village market in the Lot-et-Garonne region of France. Its glossy white, vitreous enamel coating was badly chipped, so the new owner rubbed it down with progressively finer grades of wire (steel) wool to smooth the hard edges and give the surface a soft, chalk-like patina.*

An antique Swedish *punched-tin candleholder. The tin has naturally blackened with age. However, it is possible to buy modern copies of traditional country candleholders and artificially age them with cold patining fluids.*

Copper vessels *sit on top of a folk-grained cupboard (c.1790) in a late 18th-century country house in Sweden. The pinky-red blush of the polished copper is highly prized by collectors.*

The punched-tin *door panels in this early 19th-century Pennsylvanian pie safe were designed to keep insects out, and the contents cool and aired. They feature a traditional, North American abstract floral motif.*

Fine wire-mesh *panels, rather than punched tin, are fitted in the doors of this pine storage cupboard in a wooden house in New England, USA. This allows a circulation of air and thus maximizes the shelf-life of perishable contents.*

Forerunners of the electric refrigerator, these "safes" provided cool, ventilated, and insect-repellent storage for perishable foodstuffs.

A wide range of country objects were made of iron. Apart from door hinges, locks, light fittings and – from the late 19th century – beds, most iron-made objects were to be found in the kitchen. For example, until the end of the 19th-century liquids were usually heated and meals cooked over the hearth. Iron cauldrons, pots, kettles and skillets were suspended from forged iron cranes and hooks, or supported on iron tripods, over open wood fires; the burning logs supported on andirons. The successor to open-hearth cooking – the enclosed range – was also made of (cast-) iron.

Apart from their often-decorative shapes, much of the visual charm of such metal wares lies in the surface patina that gradually builds up over time as a result of day-to-day handling, polishing and exposure to the atmosphere. Patina can range from a deep lustrous sheen (as found on highly polished copper and brass), to a dull tarnishing (as on tin) to actual corrosion. On copper and brass corrosion appears as a green-white crumbly paste, known as verdigris, and on iron as a red-brown rust.

Iron rust apart, surface patina is both aesthetically pleasing and a confirmation of the antiquity of metalwares. Consequently, manufacturers

have developed fluids for simulating it on new pieces. Known as cold patining, or antiquing, fluids, they will, almost instantly, tarnish and "age" metals. Because they are caustic and toxic, you must follow the maker's safety instructions when using these fluids (see pages 158–9). For the same reason, they should only be applied to pieces intended for display – never to items used to store or prepare liquids and foodstuffs. Also, you should never use them on genuine antiques, as they can adversely effect their value.

Antique metalwares are best cleaned and polished using commercial pastes and cleaning cloths (in accordance with the manufacturer's instructions). Brass, copper, tin and iron can then be given a protective coat of fine, white wax polish, and buffed to a sheen with a soft cloth. The exception to this is pewter, which should be dusted and then given a light buffing with a dry chamois leather.

Numerous items of plain or hand-painted, glazed or unglazed earthenware and stoneware were used in country households. Many were made from local clays by local potters, although more were "imported" from industrial areas specializing in ceramics. Also, it is surprising how international pottery is: trading links between nations touched not only coastal areas, but also many inland rural communities. Thus, blue

Left *A terra cotta storage pot with a pine lid. The design of pots such as this has remained basically unaltered for the past three centuries.*

The chalky white efflorescence *on these urns from the Tuscany region of Italy is characteristic of unglazed, weathered earthenware. It forms as a result of exposure to the atmosphere and, particularly, humidity and moisture. The greatest accumulations tend to occur in recesses and relief mouldings.*

A large terra cotta pot, *also from Tuscany, in Italy. Terra cotta is the local clay of the Tuscany region, and means, in Italian, "baked earth". Nowadays, the description terra cotta is applied around the world to virtually all types of unglazed earthenware fired from reddish-brown coloured clays.*

and white Chinese export wares appeared in Norwegian country houses, and Quimper ware from Brittany, in France, found its way to parts of lowland Scotland.

Whether new or antique, you should not attempt to artificially age pottery as you will almost certainly spoil its appearance and, as a consequence, reduce its value. To maintain tin-glazed pottery (such as maiolica, faience and delftware), lead-glazed pottery (such as creamware, majolica and Prattware), and salt-glazed pottery and stoneware, dust it regularly with a soft-bristled brush and, from time to time, wipe it over with a soft, damp cloth. Never immerse it in water for any length of time: it may eventually chip or crack because of the porosity of the glaze. If glazed pottery is particularly dirty you can add a mild liquid soap to the water before dampening the rag, but you must then rinse the piece two or three times with a clean damp rag.

To maintain unglazed antique pottery, such as terra cotta, try to restrict cleaning to regular dusting. Applying soapy water to the unglazed body may cause staining. If an unglazed piece is very dirty, just wipe down the surface with a rag slightly moistened with clean water. The only exception to the above advice on artificially ageing, and cleaning pottery is new terra cotta which can be tarnished and given a simulated coating of powdery efflorescence, using the technique described on pages 160–1.

Punched tin cabinet

During the 18th and 19th centuries it was common practice, particularly in rural communities, to store perishable foodstuffs in ventilated cabinets. These often consisted of a painted wooden frame enclosing tin panels, the latter featuring patterns and motifs made up of punched perforations. Apart from providing ventilation, such panels prevented insects getting in and shielded the contents from direct sunlight. Even after the advent of refrigeration, punched tin cabinets remained popular for some time.

WHAT YOU NEED

Metal ruler For measuring panels; positioning.

HB pencil Use with the tracing paper.

Tin sheeting Available from hardware stores. You can either cut the panels to size yourself, or have them cut by the store.

Tin snips Heavy-duty metal shears for cutting the tin panels.

Tracing paper For copying motifs and patterns.

Pair of dividers For marking circular motifs.

Graphite stick Also use with the tracing paper.

Masking tape For securing tracing paper.

Plastic goggles To protect eyes when securing tin panels with hammer and nails.

Leather gloves These are optional, but provide protection for hands when cutting the tin.

Nail punch (setter) For perforating tin panels.

Hammer A claw type, or ball-pein (ball-peen).

Wire (steel) wool Medium-grade 0.

Galvanized nails Use short, thin ones to secure tin panels to the cupboard.

Cold patining fluid (Patina green) Use type specified for iron and steel if you wish to antique the tin panels. (Optional.)

Lint-free rag Use to apply patining fluid.

Jade oil Use to arrest and fix the patina.

1   If you do not already have one, you will need to purchase a wooden cabinet which has either glazed or curtained doors and panels. If it is not already missing, remove the glass or fabric from the panels. Then, if you wish, paint the cabinet. In this case the pine carcass had already been stripped, and was therefore primed and undercoated first. Two coats of a traditional rust-red milk paint were then applied. (For more information on milk paints, see pages 62–5 and 164–9.)

2   Using a ruler, measure the dimensions of all the open panels in the cupboard. With a pencil and ruler, transfer these measurements to the sheets of tin, adding on at least 1.75cm (½in) at both ends and both sides of the panels. Then, using a pair of heavy-duty tin snips (metal shears), cut the panels to size. To ensure an accurate cut, use only the last two-thirds of the blades and carefully realign the snips with the pencil line after completing each shearing action.

3   With an HB pencil, draw the outline of the motif that you wish to appear in the panels on the tracing paper. Geometric, stylized designs tend to work best. Here, a simple flower motif was chosen, and a pair of dividers used to establish their circumference before drawing the petals freehand. The size of the motifs must be in proportion to the size of the panels. This is a matter of trial and error, so make all necessary adjustments before committing the design to the tin.

4   When you are satisfied with the drawing, and have produced a clear and accurate pencil outline, reverse the tracing paper and place it pencil-side down on a flat work surface. Then, using a thick graphite stick, rub over the back of the motif. Work diagonally and gradually build up a fairly thick coating of graphite over the entire motif. If you do not apply sufficient graphite, the outline of the motif will not completely transfer to the tin during step 5.

5   Turn the paper right-side-up (with the graphite on the underside). Use masking tape to secure the paper on top of one of the panels. Ensure the middle of the motif is directly over the middle of the panel. (Find the middle of a panel by drawing two lines between the diagonally opposite corners; the middle is where they intersect.) Then, pressing firmly, go over the outline of the motif with the HB pencil. Remove the paper to reveal the outline on the tin.

6   Lay the tin flat on a hard work surface. Position the tip of a nail punch on the outline, and strike the head of the punch firmly with a hammer. Repeat at short intervals around the rest of the outline. If the cabinet is purely decorative, you do not have to perforate the tin. Be consistent – make the blows either all perforations or all indentations. Attach the panels to the inside of the cabinet with short, thin galvanized nails. If you wish to "age" the tin see pages 158–9.

Patining metals

Objects made from bronze, brass and copper will become tarnished, and to some degree corroded, over the years through everyday use and exposure to the atmosphere. The chemical reactions produced by oxidization on their surface gradually result in a patina that is both aesthetically pleasing and a confirmation of age. Fortunately, it is very easy to reproduce this lengthy natural process in a matter of minutes using cold patining fluids. However, you must refer to the advice on safety (opposite), before proceeding.

WHAT YOU NEED

Plastic goggles To protect your eyes.

Face mask To minimize inhalation of vapour from patining fluid.

Household rubber gloves Purchase chemical-resistant ones to protect skin from patining fluid.

Plastic sheeting To protect the work surface.

Blunt knife For scraping off old wax.

Salt and vinegar A tablespoon of the former and a small bottle of the latter.

Wire (steel) wool Fine grade 000.

Towelling (terrycloth) For drying metals prior to patining.

Lint-free rag For applying the fluid and oil.

White spirit (mineral spirits) Small bottle.

Lacquer solvent Small bottle, only required if you need to remove lacquer from new brass prior to patining.

Cold patining fluid (Patina green) Small bottle of type specified for brass/copper.

Old glass jar For decanting the patining fluid.

Jade oil Small bottle of this fixitive, to arrest and fix the patining process.

Brushes Either a 2.5cm (1in) standard decorator's brush, or a 1.75cm (½in) artist's brush, for applying patining fluid.

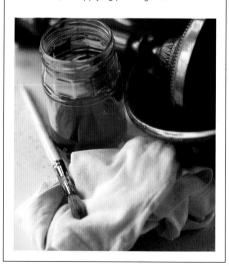

Cold patining fluids are available from artist's suppliers and some craft stores. They are made in a variety of formulations. The most commonly used type is designed to age brass, bronze and copper (demonstrated here on bronze candlesticks and copper bowls). A patining fluid for ageing iron, steel and tin is also available. It has the same method of application, and is shown on the punched tin panels on page 156.

Before using cold patining fluids it is very important to note that they are toxic and corrosive (most contain nitric acid). They can cause irritation if they come into contact with eyes and skin, can be harmful if inhaled, and will poison to varying degrees if you accidently swallow them. Consequently, when handling them you must work in a well-ventilated area, wear plastic goggles, a face mask and chemical-resistant rubber gloves and, most important of all, keep children and pets well out of the way.

Patining bronze

1 Scrape off wax on old candlesticks with the blunt edge of a knife. Remove the rest (plus any dirt) by soaking in very hot soapy water, and gently rubbing with grade 00 wire (steel) wool. Rinse with clean water, and dry with towelling (terrycloth). To remove any oily deposits, gently rub down with lint-free rag moistened with white spirit (mineral spirits). Remove lacquer from new brass with a rag dipped in a commercial lacquer solvent.

2 Brush on the patining fluid. A chemical reaction will occur on the surface, turning bronze dark brown and brass a greeny-black-brown. Apply more fluid if you wish: the more you apply and the longer you leave it, the darker the colour. After 24 hours, bronze and brass will also develop a blue-green tinge. To fix the finish, rinse under cold water, dry with towelling (terrycloth), brush on jade oil, and dry as before.

Patining copper

The patining process *on the copper bowl and plate (above) and the bronze candlesticks (opposite) was fixed with jade oil after 4 hours. Darker patina, with a verdigris-like blue-green tinge, can be achieved by delaying fixing for 24 hours.*

1 To prepare the surfaces of the copper bowls you must first remove any dirt or grease. Begin by mixing a cleaning solution consisting of: one tablespoon of salt, one tablespoon of vinegar, and half a pint of hot water. Next, gently rub this over the surface of the copper with fine grade 000 wire (steel) wool. Then wash the bowls in warm soapy water with lint-free rag. Finally, rinse with cold water, and dry with towelling (terrycloth).

2 Wipe on the patining fluid with lint-free rag. The chemical reaction will be rapid: the copper will develop a patchy, dull brown-black hue within minutes, and some areas will show a blue-green tinge after 24 hours. You will rarely need to apply more fluid, other than to even up the patina. If you wish to reduce the degree of patina, gently rub it down with fine grade 000 wire (steel) wool. Fix finish as described in step 2 of Patining bronze (above).

Weathered terra cotta

A mixture of sand and clay, reddish-brown in colour and traditionally unglazed, terra cotta is one of the most common forms of earthenware found in rural communities. Used for storage vessels, sculpture and as a decorative building material, one of its main attractions is the way in which it gradually changes in appearance as a result of exposure to the elements. An uneven darkening of colour, and the growth of an off-white, powdery surface crust, can be duplicated with paints and powders, using the following technique.

WHAT YOU NEED

White matte emulsion (latex) paint The main ingredient of the weathering glaze. You will need less than half a glass (jam) jar full.

Universal stainers You will need small bottles of raw umber and black.

Acrylic emulsion (latex) glaze Try to buy the slow-setting type as this will delay the drying time of the weathering glaze, and allow you more time to sprinkle on the powder (see below). Only a very small quantity is needed, even for a fairly large pot.

Small pointing trowel Can be used to blend the glaze and the dry powders.

Artist's palette This provides an ideal surface for mixing small quantities of glaze, as well as blending powders. You can use small mixing containers instead, if you prefer.

Standard decorator's brush You will need a 7.5–15cm (3–6in) brush, depending on the size of the pot, for applying the glaze.

Tablespoon Use to sprinkle on the powder.

Whiting (powdered chalk/limestone) A white, chalky powder. You only need to buy the smallest bag available.

Rottenstone A light gray-coloured powder. Again, buy the smallest bag available.

Lint-free rag Use for rubbing in the powder, and wiping off excess powder.

1 You can purchase both glazed and unglazed terra cotta pots and vases. It is preferable to buy the unglazed type for this project, as the glaze that you apply in step 3 will adhere to its surface more easily. If you intend to weather a pot that has already been used, wash it thoroughly with water and then apply a mild fungicide solution prior to drying. The fungicide will minimize the risk of future mould growth, which would probably lift off the weathering glaze at a later date.

2 You will need only a small quantity of glaze to cover even a largish pot. About 0.125 litre (¼ pint/½ US cup) should suffice. Mix the ingredients in a ratio of: 75 percent white matte emulsion (latex) paint, 15 percent raw umber universal stainer, 5 percent black universal stainer, and 5 percent acrylic emulsion (latex) glaze. These can be mixed in a small container or on an artist's palette. Palettes made up of disposable, waterproof sheets of paper are ideal.

3 Work the glaze into the surface of the pot, using a medium or large standard decorator's brush. A new, unglazed terra cotta pot will be very absorbent. Consequently, you will almost certainly have to apply two or three coats of glaze, waiting for each one to become tacky before applying the next. When you start brushing on the final coat, work as quickly as you can, proceeding to steps 4 and 5 as soon as possible (while the glaze is still tacky and before it dries).

4 Blend together one tablespoon each of whiting and rottenstone. Again, you can either do this on an artist's palette or in a small mixing container. The resulting mix will be slightly off-white in colour, and will have the appearance of the efflorescence that gradually forms on terra cotta as a result of alternating exposure to damp and heat. (If you are concerned that you will not be able to blend the powders before the weathering glaze dries, blend the powders prior to step 3.)

5 Using the tablespoon, sprinkle the powders over the tacky surface of the pot. You will need to turn the pot around, and partly on its side, to achieve a sufficient build-up of powder. For the most effective results, sprinkle thicker deposits in the recessed areas around the rim, and on the upper parts of the decorative moulding on the sides. These are the areas that tend to show a greater accumulation of efflorescence when a terra cotta vessel weathers naturally.

6 Leave the pot for 2 hours, while the underlying glaze dries out. Then, using a lint-free rag or a standard decorator's brush (or both), wipe off any excess powder. Do not apply too much pressure, and leave some loose powder in the recessed areas of the mouldings. This will produce a more realistic finish. If necessary, brush on more powder. It will not adhere permanently because the glaze has dried, but it will add to the chalky appearance of the terra cotta.

Above and left *Very few specialist tools are required to produce the decorative finishes and effects illustrated in this book. The badger softener (left) used for vinegar graining, and the artist's flogger (above) used for oak graining, are two examples and, although more expensive than standard brushes, are well worth the investment.*

The basics

THIS SECTION LISTS AND DESCRIBES THE TOOLS AND MATERIALS YOU WILL NEED TO reproduce the decorative finishes and effects shown throughout the book. It also includes instructions on how to prepare different types of surfaces for decoration, how to tint and mix paints and glazes, and how to clean brushes properly to maximize their longevity. Most importantly, there is some basic information on safety. A few of the materials listed can be potentially harmful if handled incorrectly. So, to protect your health you must follow the advice given here, together with any specific instructions provided by the product's manufacturer.

Tools & equipment

Artist's brushes
Fine-tipped types are available in a range of sizes and qualities. Sable-bristled ones are the best for freehand work, such as folk painting.

Artist's palette
Made from either varnished wood, plastic, or layers of disposable waterproof paper. Provides an ideal surface for mixing small quantities of powder pigments and artist's oils.

Badger and hog's hair softeners
There are two qualities of artist's softening brushes available: badger hair and hog's hair. Available in a range of sizes, both are used to soften and blend marks and patterns made in still-wet (or tacky) glazes, such as when folk graining or marbling. Although more expensive, badger softeners have finer bristles and produce a more subtle finish than hog's hair.

Combing tools
The combs used to drag through wet glazes to simulate the figuring of wood when folk graining are made from oiled card, rubber, plastic or steel, and are available in a range of sizes.

Compasses
A small pair of compasses will help you to outline circular motifs when designing your own motifs for stencilling and punching tin.

Craft knives
The type of craft knife featuring retractable, disposable blades can be used as an alternative to a scalpel when cutting out stencils. Also useful for trimming masking tape.

Cutting board
A wooden or plastic cutting board (the type used in a kitchen) will protect your work surface from damage when cutting out stencils.

Dust sheets
Cotton and plastic dust sheets (or old newspapers) are essential for protecting the work surface, floor and surrounding areas and objects when preparing surfaces and applying paints and glazes.

Dusting brushes
Also known as jamb dusters, soft-bristled dusting brushes are available in various sizes. They are designed to remove dust from surfaces prior to painting, glazing and varnishing.

Erasers
For the removal of pencil marks and outlines after completing decorative finishes such as border stencils and punched tin panelling.

Face masks
See the section on Safety (page 169).

Floggers
Coarse, long-bristled artist's flogging brushes are available in a range of sizes. Use for tapping up and down wet glazes to simulate oak grain.

Floor sander
To prepare old wooden floorboards for liming, hire or rent a commercial floor-sanding machine. They come with various grades (grits) of sandpaper (in disposable sheet form).

Galvanized nails
Use these rust-proofed nails to attach sheets of punched tin to carcass furniture.

Graphite stick
A thick-tipped, soft lead pencil available from artist's suppliers. Rub it over the back of tracing paper when transferring the outline of motifs and patterns to sheets of stencil card.

Hammer
Use a ball-pein (ball-peen) or small carpenter's hammer to drive galvanized nails into carcass furniture when securing punched-tin panels.

Hot air stripper gun
Use an electric stripper gun when distressing painted surfaces. Do not use a gas-powered blowtorch, as it is difficult to control and its naked flame can damage the underlying wood.

Lining paper
Line uneven plaster walls with sheets of thick (heavy-gauge) lining paper, prior to decorating.

When using to sketch designs, brown packing paper can be substituted.

Lint-free rag
Unlike ordinary rags, these don't deposit small pieces of fibre on bristles or wet glazes when decorating, and thus spoil the finished work.

Masking tape
Use to protect surrounding surfaces from paints and glazes, and to secure stencil cards in position while working. The "low-tack" type tends not to pull off background finishes.

Mixing containers
A large plastic bucket with a capacity of 10 litres (2 gallons) is needed for soaking animal glue overnight (before making it into a liming mixture), and mixing or decanting large quantities of undercoats and basecoats. You will also need five or six plastic or alloy paint kettles for mixing paints and glazes. The most useful sizes have a capacity of 1–2 litres (1¾–3 UK pints/1–2 US quarts). Old glass jars and small saucers are useful for mixing small quantities.

Mottlers (spalters)
Specialist brushes that are dragged through wet glazes to simulate wood grain. Available from artist's suppliers, they have either sable, hog's hair, or squirrel hair bristles.

Nail punch
Use with a hammer to drive nail heads below the surface of floorboards prior to liming.

Palette knives
Purchase two or three of these from an artist's suppliers, and use to mix powder pigments and small quantities of glaze on an artist's palette.

Pencils
HB grade pencils are best for drawing or tracing the outlines of motifs and patterns. Use with a spirit level to mark true horizontals or verticals on walls before border stencilling.

Plastic goggles
See the section on Safety (page 169).

Pointing trowel
A small builder's pointing trowel can be useful for mixing various powders into glazes.

Protective gloves
See the section on Safety (page 169).

Razor blades
Use the safety-back type (from drug stores) for distressing paintwork on furniture.

Sandpaper
Coarse, medium and fine grades (grits). Use for smoothing surfaces prior to decoration, and distressing paints and glazes when antiquing.

Scalpel
For cutting out motifs/patterns in stencil card.

Silicon carbide paper (wet-and-dry paper)
A range of grades (grits) available. Use coarser grades dry or with water to key painted surfaces before painting/glazing. Use finer grades for smoothing surfaces.

Spoons
Wooden stirring spoons, or alloy tablespoons are useful for mixing large quantities of paints and glazes, and measuring out quantities of powder pigments, mediums and solvents.

Spirit level
Use a large size for marking out true horizontal lines around walls when border stencilling.

Standard decorator's brushes
Available from hardware stores in sizes ranging from 1.25cm (½in) to 15cm (6in), they are mainly used to apply primers, undercoats, eggshell and emulsion (latex) paints.

Steel spatula
Use to remove old wallpaper and damaged plaster when preparing surfaces.

Steel ruler (measure)
Provides a solid edge to work against when cutting straight lines in stencil card.

Stencil brushes
Stiff-bristled, round brushes, available from craft stores – specifically designed for stencilling work (only holding a small quantity of paint or glaze at a time, which encourages a controlled build-up of colour and reduces risk of paint or glaze creeping behind stencil card).

Tin snips (metal shears)
Heavy-duty metal shears available from hardware stores. For cutting sheets of punched tin.

Towelling (terrycloth)
Clean, absorbent, old towels are very useful for drying surfaces prior to decorating.

Tracing paper
Use semi-transparent sheets of tracing paper to copy and transfer the outlines of motifs and patterns from source material to stencil card.

Varnishing brushes
Use good-quality standard decorating brushes to apply protective coats of varnish. However, fine-bristled varnishing brushes ("gliders") produce a smoother, brushmark-free finish.

Wire (steel) wool
Available in grades: 0000–3. Use the finest when applying polishes and cutting back the sheen of underlying glazes and varnishes. The coarsest are useful for distressing paintwork.

Materials

Acrylic emulsion (latex) glaze
Water-based glaze, available from artist's suppliers. Made from PVA adhesive and water, it is white in the tin, but sets clear. Provides a protective finish that will not yellow with age or darken underlying colours.

Artist's acrylics (latex paints)
Available in small tubes in a range of colours. Solvent in water, they can be used as paints or glazes in their own right, or for tinting white emulsion (latex) paints. Quick to dry, they are useful for applying rapid overlays of colour.

Artist's intenso colours
These highly concentrated pigments are available in liquid form, and are most useful for tinting large quantities of white paint.

Artist's oil paints
Available in tube form, they are made up of pigment and linseed oil. Can be mixed with transparent oil glaze and white spirits (mineral spirits) to produce glazes of varying translucency. Can also be used to tint white oil-based paints, such as undercoat and eggshell.

Button polish
Type of shellac or French polish with most of the impurities removed. Applied with a lint-free cotton pad, it will produce a protective, deep, lustrous sheen on stained wooden furniture.

Cold patining fluids
Available from some artist's suppliers and craft stores in a variety of formulations. Some are designed to rapidly age or antique brass, bronze and copper; others to give a patina to iron and steel. They contain nitric acid, so are highly corrosive and must be used with care. (See the section on Safety, page 169).

Eggshell paints
Oil-based paints, available in a range of colours, that dry to a mid-sheen finish. Mainly used to create smooth, opaque basecoats, over which semi-translucent glazes can be applied.

Emulsion (latex) paints
Water-based paints, available in a range of colours and finishes (matte and mid-sheen). The white versions can be tinted with universal stainers and powder pigments. Can be used as basecoats for semi-translucent glazes, or thinned with water to make glazes and washes.

Fuller's earth

A brown-gray coloured powder available from artist's suppliers. Use, where specified, to stabilize certain glazes. Apply by wiping it over the underlying basecoat with a damp, lint-free rag.

Furniture waxes

Various types of commercial furniture wax are available. Beeswax-based versions are best. Clear waxes will protect a painted finish, and when buffed with a rag produce a soft, lustrous sheen over the surface. Tinted waxes do much the same, although they also darken, enrich and, to some extent, artificially age (or antique) underlying colours.

Jade oil

Available from suppliers of cold-patining fluids. Used to arrest the chemical reaction produced on the surface of metals and alloys by patining fluids. It will also fix the finish.

Knotting compound

Use this shellac-based liquid to seal knots in bare wood prior to decorating, and prevent resin seeping out and lifting off paintwork or varnish. Available in both brown and white.

Metal paints

Hardware shops and artist's suppliers sell a type of commercial paint specifically formulated for metal surfaces. Does not need a primer or undercoat when applied to bare metal. Contains ingredients that neutralize and bind rust on iron and steel.

Metallic powders

Fine powders, available from artist's suppliers in colours ranging from antique gold and gold to silver, bronze, copper and platinum. Can be mixed into glazes to produce metallic paints.

Methylated spirits (denatured alcohol)

Can be used to dilute or dissolve shellac, and distress wet or dry emulsion (latex) paints.

Milk paint (buttermilk or casein paint)

Traditionally made during the 18th and 19th centuries by mixing earth-coloured pigments with buttermilk or skimmed milk, plus a little lime (the latter acts as an insecticide and a fungicide). Dries to a smooth finish, somewhere between matte and mid-sheen, and subtly mellows with age. Some companies (see Directory, pages 172–3) still manufacture milk paint in a range of colours that match those found on 18th- and 19th-century furniture, joinery and plasterwork. It is also possible to buy casein paint in powder form from specialist paint suppliers, and mix it yourself: tinting with artist's powder pigments or universal stainers, and diluting with water.

Paint strippers

Commercial paint-stripping fluids will remove old paint and varnish from wooden and metal surfaces. They are highly caustic (and give off unpleasant fumes), so always work in a well-ventilated area and wear plastic goggles, chemical-resistant gloves and a face mask, to protect your eyes, skin and lungs. Avoid the water-based type of stripper when working on wooden surfaces, as it will raise the grain.

Plaster filler (spackle)

Commercial cellulose filler is used to repair small sections of damaged plaster prior to re-decorating. Buy ready-mixed, or in powder form (which you mix to a paste with water).

Powder pigments

Available from artist's suppliers. Solvent in water, they come in a wide range of natural or chemically manufactured colours. They can be mixed with water to form glazes and washes, or used to tint white emulsion (latex) paint.

Pre-sized canvas

Heavy duty canvas, which has been pre-sized (pre-sealed) for painting, is available in various widths from many large stores and craft shops. Can be used as a floorcloth, and makes an ideal base for painting and stencilling.

Primer/undercoats

Combined primer/undercoat paints can be water- or oil-based. Use to seal and cover bare wood prior to applying eggshell paint.

Rottenstone

A fine, gray-coloured limestone powder that can be sprinkled over a tacky glaze to simulate efflorescence on stonework and ceramics. It can also be mixed with a little lemon juice to create a mildly abrasive paste for cutting back and polishing varnished surfaces.

Stencil card

Available in sheet form from craft stores/artist's suppliers. Cut out the outlines of motifs and patterns in it to make your own stencils.

Transparent oil (scumble) glaze

White or honey-coloured liquid; colourless if thinned with white spirit (mineral spirits) and brushed out over a surface. Can be tinted with artist's oils, universal stainers or oil-based paints, and thinned with white spirit (mineral spirits) for a translucent oil-based glaze.

Universal stainers

Concentrated, pre-mixed chemical dyes, available from artist's suppliers, and used to tint glazes and white paint. Solvent in white spirit (mineral spirits), they produce cruder colours than artist's oils, and need to be heavily diluted.

Varnishes

Clear polyurethane varnishes protect finishes against moisture, wear and tear, heat and alcohol. Available in matte, mid-sheen and gloss types. They enrich underlying colours, but have a tendency to yellow with age (although manufacturers are gradually overcoming this).

Varnish strippers

Commercial varnish-stripping fluids have similar properties to paint strippers (see above), so take the same precautions when using them.

White spirit (mineral spirits)

Also known as turpentine substitute. A solvent used to dilute oil-based paints and glazes and varnishes. Also use to clean brushes.

White vinegar (acetic acid)

Use ordinary household vinegar to produce a localized "cissing" effect.

Whiting (ground chalk)

Fine white powder, available from artist's suppliers. Use it to add body to water-based glazes or to simulate efflorescence on stoneware.

Preparing surfaces

Bare plaster

To prepare bare plaster for decorating, proceed as follows:

- Scrape out loose ("live") patches of old plaster with a steel spatula.
- Chamfer the edges of the holes with coarse- or medium-grade (grit) sandpaper.
- Brush off any plaster dust with an old standard decorator's brush.
- Dampen the holes and the surrounding areas by brushing on a little water.
- Fill the holes with a commercial cellulose plaster filler (spackle) in accordance with the manufacturer's instructions, using a steel spatula or pointing trowel. The filler should stand just proud of, and slightly overlap, the surrounding surface. Then leave the filler to dry thoroughly.
- Level off with medium-grade sandpaper.
- Fill any minor cracks with fine-grade cellulose plaster filler (spackle). Leave to dry.
- Smooth all repairs, plus the entire surface, with fine-grade (grit) sandpaper.
- If the plaster is to be covered with lining paper, seal it first with a coat of emulsion (latex) glaze that is well diluted with water.
- If you are using a water-based paint as the basecoat for the decorative finish, this can now be brushed straight onto the plaster (or lining paper on top).
- If you are using an oil-based paint (such as eggshell) as the basecoat for the decorative finish, first seal the surface with an oil-based primer, and allow to dry. Then apply an oil-based undercoat, and leave to dry.

Bare wood

To prepare bare or untreated wood for painting, proceed as follows:

- Smooth down the surface with fine-grade (grit) sandpaper.
- Cover any knots in the wood with two coats of white knotting compound.
- Cover any exposed nail or screw heads with two coats of metal primer.
- Fill any holes with a commercial, flexible wood filler (spackle). Leave to dry.
- Level off filler with medium-grade (grit) sandpaper.

- Smooth down repaired areas (and rest of wooden surface) with fine-grade sandpaper.
Note: If you want a very smooth surface for painting, apply a thin layer of cellulose filler (spackle), and smooth down with medium- and then fine-grade (grit) sandpaper (see Combing a trunk, pages 130–1).
- If you intend to apply an oil-based basecoat (such as eggshell paint) for the decorative finish, first brush on a coat of oil-based primer, and leave to dry. Then brush on one or two coats of oil-based undercoat.
- If you intend to apply milk paint, use a water-based primer.

Lining paper

To prepare plaster walls that have been covered with new lining paper, proceed as follows:

- If you intend to apply a water-based basecoat, first brush on a thin wash of emulsion (latex) paint (diluted half and half with water) to seal the surface. Leave to dry, then apply one or two coats of the basecoat.
- If you intend to apply an oil-based basecoat (such as eggshell paint), brush on an oil-based primer that has been diluted 2:1 with white spirit (mineral spirits). Then apply one or two coats of oil-based undercoat.

Metals

If you wish to remove paint from metal or alloy surfaces prior to re-painting or antiquing with cold patining fluids, proceed as follows:

- Make sure that the work area is well ventilated, and that the work surface is covered with plastic sheeting.
- Put on protective plastic goggles, face mask and chemical-resistant rubber gloves.
- Brush on several coats of a commercial spirit-based paint stripper.
- As the paint begins to blister, rub it with coarse grade (3) wire (steel) wool. Apply more coats of paint stripper if necessary and repeat.
- Neutralize any residue of stripper left on the surface by rubbing it down with a rag soaked in white spirit (mineral spirits).

If you intend to apply cold patining fluid, proceed as described and illustrated on pages 158–9. If you intend to apply a commercial metal paint (with a built-in rust converter and stabilizer), apply straight from the can. If you intend to apply an ordinary oil-based topcoat to bare metal that has been stripped of paint (as above), or bare metal that has never been painted, proceed as follows:

- Rub off any surface rust with coarse or medium-grade (3 or 1) wire (steel) wool, and then a clean rag.
- Brush on one coat of a commercial metal primer, and allow to dry.
- Brush on one or two coats of an oil-based undercoat.

Painted plaster

To prepare plaster that has already been painted (and the paintwork is sound) proceed as follows:

- If the painted surface is sound, wash it down with a rag and warm soapy water (and a little disinfectant) to remove any dirt. Treat any mould with a commercial fungicide.
- If the paint is oil-based gloss or eggshell, key the surface by rubbing it down with coarse or medium-grade (grit) wet-and-dry paper.
- If the decorative finish requires an oil-based basecoat, brush on an oil-based undercoat (in the appropriate colour).
- If the decorative finish requires an emulsion (latex) paint basecoat, apply this directly on top of the old painted finish. However, you should note that sometimes the pigments (particularly reds) used in some older paints can be unstable, and have a tendency to bleed through emulsion (latex) paints applied directly on top of them.
Note: If you think that this a possibility, you should apply one or two coats of a commercial aluminium primer after cleaning and keying the surface.

To prepare plaster that has already been painted, but where the paintwork is flaking or bubbling off, proceed as follows:

- Clean as above, then rub down with medium-grade (grit) sandpaper.

- Apply a commercial surface sealer, and leave to dry.
- Level out any surface irregularities with fine-grade cellulose filler (spackle), and allow to dry.
- Smooth any repairs with fine-grade (grit) sandpaper or wet-and-dry paper.
- If the decorative finish requires an oil-based basecoat (eggshell), brush on an oil-based undercoat in the appropriate colour.
- If the decorative finish requires an emulsion (latex) paint undercoat, apply directly onto the surface.

Note: If a painted plaster surface is in particularly bad condition, it is often advisable to cover it with lining paper before applying the decorative finish.

Painted wood

To prepare already painted wooden surfaces for painted decoration, use the same method outlined above for preparing painted plaster. To completely remove paint from wooden surfaces prior to decorating, proceed as follows:

- Open all windows and doors to make sure that the work area is well-ventilated.

- Cover the work surface and surrounding areas with plastic sheeting.
- Put on protective plastic goggles, face mask and chemical-resistant gloves.
- Brush on several coats of a commercial spirit-based paint stripper. Do not use a water-based stripper, as this will raise the grain of the underlying wood.
- As it begins to bubble and flake up, scrape off the paint with a steel spatula and grade 0 wire (steel) wool. Always work in the direction of the grain, and use a small wire brush to remove paint from recessed areas.
- To neutralize the stripper, rub down the exposed wood with a rag soaked in white spirit (mineral spirits).
- Smooth down the surface with fine-grade (grit) sandpaper.

Shellacked and varnished wood

Provided they are in good condition, prepare shellacked and varnished surfaces for painting by cleaning and keying using the same method as described for preparing painted wooden surfaces (see above). However, if the surface is flaking or friable, proceed as follows:

- Remove shellac by dissolving it with methylated spirits (denatured alcohol) and fine-grade (00) wire (steel) wool. Wipe off the residue with lint-free cotton rag.
- Remove flaking cellulose varnish with a commercial paint stripper, as described under preparing painted wood. Remember to neutralize any residue of the stripper left on the surface by rubbing down with a rag soaked in white spirit (mineral spirits).
- Remove all other types of varnish with a commercial varnish stripper. Remember to neutralize afterwards, as described immediately above.

Waxed and oiled wood

To prepare waxed or oiled wood for painting, proceed as follows:

- Gently rub down the surface in the direction of the grain with white spirit (mineral spirits) and fine-grade wire (steel) wool.
- When the wax or oil begins to dissolve, continue rubbing down the surface with a clean rag soaked in white spirit (mineral spirits).
- Now follow the instructions for preparing bare wood for painting.

Mixing paints & glazes

Oil-based paints

Oil-based eggshell paints can be purchased already mixed in the required colour. Alternatively, you can mix your own to the required colour by tinting white eggshell paint with artist's oils or universal stainers. You do this quite simply by slowly mixing in the pigments until you have achieved the desired colour.

Oil-based glazes

Glazes are made up of pigments suspended in a clear medium and sufficiently thinned with a solvent to make them semi-translucent when applied over an opaque basecoat. The tinted, semi-translucent glaze allows the underlying base colour to "ghost" through it, creating subtle combinations, and gradations of colour.

The simplest way to make an oil-based glaze is to tint eggshell paint with pigment (artist's oils, universal stainers, etc) and then thin it with white spirit (mineral spirits) so that it

becomes increasingly less opaque and more translucent. More subtle oil-based glazes are created by mixing pigments with transparent oil glaze and white spirit (mineral spirits).

The recipes given throughout the book for oil-based glazes include the approximate proportions of each pigment in relation to the proportions of medium (transparent oil glaze) and solvent (white spirit/mineral spirits). For example, the first spattering glaze for the Faux Porphyry finish (page 114) is 50 percent burnt sienna artist's oil; 30 percent transparent oil glaze; 20 percent white spirit (mineral spirits). It is difficult to specify the total quantity of glaze required, as this depends on the absorbency of the underlying surface and how thickly you apply the glaze. However, a rough rule-of-thumb is: 1 litre (1¼ UK pints/1 US quart) of glaze to cover about 30 sq. metres (33 sq. yards) of surface. So, for example, if you wanted to mix 1 litre (1¼ UK pints/1 US quart)

of the first spattering glaze for faux porphyry, you should proceed as follows:

- Using a clean old brush or a spoon, blend together in a mixing container 0.3 litres (½ UK pint/⅓ US quart) of transparent oil glaze and 0.2 litres (⅓ pint/1 US cup) of white spirit (mineral spirits).
- Pour off a small quantity of this mixture into a second container.
- Very gradually blend the burnt sienna artist's oil into the mixture in the second container. Keep going until you have added 0.5 litres (1 pint/½ US quart) of artist's oil.
- Slowly blend the creamy, coloured mixture in the second container into the medium and solvent in the first container.

Having mixed the glaze, now swatch a little of it out over the faux porphyry basecoat to check that the colour and the degree of translucency matches the spatter shown in the step-by-step picture. To increase the translucency of the glaze, add some more transparent oil glaze and white spirit (mineral spirits). If you wish to increase the opacity of the glaze, add more pigment (artist's oil).

This example shows you how to mix a large quantity of glaze. However, the principles of mixing are the same for smaller quantities: scale down the quantities, but keep their recommended proportions the same.

Water-based paints and glazes

Water-based paints, such as commercial emulsions (latex paints) and artist's acrylics, can be bought ready-mixed in the required colour. Or, mix your own by tinting white emulsion (latex) paint with pigments (artist's acrylics, universal stainers, or artist's powder pigments). To make water-based glazes and washes, adopt the same principle as when mixing oil-based glazes. The only differences are: first, the solvent used is water (not white spirit/mineral spirits); second, when using artist's powder pigments dissolve them in a little water before adding them the diluted paint, rather than blending them in dry from the packet. Third, you do not use a medium, such as transparent oil glaze.

Cleaning brushes

To remove oil-based paints, glazes and varnishes from brushes, proceed as follows:

1 Wipe off and squeeze out excess paint on spare pieces of lining paper.

2 Thoroughly clean the bristles in a container of white spirit (mineral spirits) or a commercial brush cleaner (some of which are specifically designed to dissolve polyurethane varnish). Keep changing the spirits as and when necessary, until all traces of colour have been removed from the bristles. Also, try to avoid getting spirits into the stock of the brush, as this will eventually result in the bristles dropping out. (For this reason, you should try to avoid getting paint, glaze or varnish into the stock in the first place.)

3 When all the paint, glaze or varnish has been removed, rinse the bristles thoroughly under cold running water.

4 Remove as much of the water as possible by shaking the brush vigorously.

5 Fold a plain sheet of paper around the bristles, and hold it in place with an elastic band wound around the stock. (This will stop the bristles splaying out as they dry.)

6 Lay the brush on its side, or support it bristles-up. Leave it to dry slowly at room temperature (and away from direct heat).

To remove water-based paints, glazes and varnishes from brushes, proceed as follows:

1 Clean the brush as soon as possible after use in a weak solution of mild soap and water. Do not use detergents as they will strip the bristles of their natural oils.

2 Once all traces of paint, glaze or varnish have been removed, follow steps 3–6 above.

Safety

Some of the materials you will be using to create country finishes are either toxic, flammable, or both. The manufacturers of such products are almost invariably required by law to provide warnings to that effect on the container the product is supplied in. You should always heed these warnings, together with the accompanying advice and instructions on handling.

Over and above any specific instructions supplied by the manufacturer, it is important that you always adopt the following basic safety measures to protect your health:

- Always keep a first-aid kit close to hand.
- Work in a well-ventilated area. In other words, wherever possible keep any doors and windows open to allow a free-flow of air.
- Always keep any flammable products well away from naked flames and intense sources of heat – in particular, electric fires and central heating radiators.

- Keep children and pets out of the work area at all times.
- Protect your eyes from dust and accidental splashes of fluid by wearing plastic goggles. These are available from most good hardware stores.
- Protect your face and lungs from dust, accidental splashes and noxious vapours by wearing a respiratory (or dust) mask.
- Protect your hands from caustic fluids by wearing rubber (household) gloves or, better still, chemical-resistant gloves. The chemical-resistant type are available from many specialist decorating suppliers.

- Wear old clothes or decorator's overalls.
- Cover work surfaces and surrounding areas with plastic or heavy-duty cotton dust sheets (or, at the very least, sheets of old newspaper).
- Never store old rags that have been impregnated with solvents, such as white spirit (mineral spirits) or methylated spirits (denatured alcohol), in plastic bags. They have been known to spontaneously combust under these circumstances.
- Seek out immediate medical advice if you accidentally swallow any fluids or powders, or get them in your eyes.
- Take extra care when using sharp cutting tools, such as crafts knives, razor blades, scalpels and tin snips (metal shears).

The Directory

BRITAIN

Paints and materials

J. W. Bollom Group
PO Box 76
Croydon Road
Beckenham
Kent BR3 4BL
Manufacturers and suppliers of a wide range of paints, varnishes, stains, waxes and specialist decorating equipment.

C. Brewer
327 Putney Bridge Road
London SW15 2PG
Suppliers of a wide range of decorating materials and equipment.

Lawrence T. Bridgeman
No.1 Church Road
Roberttown
West Yorkshire WF15 7LS
Suppliers of traditional milk paints and oil paints, incorporating pigments used since 1816, and in colours authentic to Colonial, Federal and Victorian architecture and interiors.

Brodie and Middleton Ltd
68 Drury Lane
London WC2B 5SP
Suppliers of decorating brushes, metallic powders, paints, pigments and powder colours.

H. J. Chard and Son
Albert Road
Bristol BS2 0XS
Suppliers of traditional lime-washes, plasters and renders.

Cole & Son Ltd
18 Mortimer Street
London W1A 4BU
Suppliers of a range of period paints.

Cornelissen & Son Ltd
105 Great Russell Street
London WC1B 3RY
Specialists in period-style paints and powder pigments.

Craig and Rose plc
172 Leith Walk
Edinburgh EH6 5EP
Manufacturers and suppliers of traditional oil- and spirit-based varnishes.

Crown Berger Europe Ltd
PO Box 37
Crown House
Hollins Road
Darwen
Lancashire BB3 0BG
Manufacturers of a wide range of interior and exterior paints.

Daler-Rowney Ltd
12 Percy Street
London W1A 2BP
Manufacturers and suppliers of a wide range of artist's materials.

Farrow & Ball Ltd
33 Uddens Trading Estate
Wimborne
Dorset BH21 7NL
Suppliers of traditional paints. In addition, they also carry the National Trust paint range, which includes 57 colourways.

Fired Earth plc
Twyford Mill
Oxford Road
Adderbury
Oxfordshire OX17 3HP

Also at:
21 Battersea Square
London SW11 3JF
Also at:
102 Portland Road
London W11 4LX
Suppliers of a wide range of traditional paint colours, notably those suitable for 19th-century interiors.

Green & Stone
259 King's Road
London SW3 5EL

Also at:
1 North House
North Street
Chichester PO19 1HE
Suppliers of a wide range of specialist decorating materials, including pre-cut stencils and stencil card.

Greenham Trading
Telford Place
Crawley
West Sussex RH10 2TP
Suppliers of Solvex chemical-resistant gloves.

A. S. Handover Ltd
37 Mildmay Grove
London N1 4RH
Suppliers of artists' brushes and specialist decorating materials.

Heart of the Country
Home Farm
Swinsen
Near Litchfield
Staffordshire S14 9QR
Specialists in American period-style paints.

House of Harbru
Unit 3, Cuba Industrial Estate
Bolton Road North
Ramsbottom BL0 0NE
Suppliers of wax polishes, oils, and wood stains.

John T. Keep & Sons Ltd
15 Theobald's Road
London WC1X 8FN
Suppliers of varnishes, transparent oil glaze and universal stainers.

Liberon Waxes
Mountfield Industrial Estate
Learoyd Road
New Romney
Kent TN28 8XU
Suppliers of waxes, polishes and cold patining fluids.

Nutshell Natural Paints
New Take
Staverton
Devon TQ9 6PE
Suppliers of paints and a wide range of powder pigments.

Omnihome Ltd
77 Goldbourne Road
London W10 5NP
Suppliers of artist's brushes, oil colours and varnishes.

Paint Library
25 Draycott Place
London SW3 2SH
Suppliers of paints, powder pigments and universal stainers.

Papers and Paints
4 Park Walk
London SW10 0AD
Suppliers of specialist paints, including a range of "historic" colours, and decorating materials. They also offer a colour-matching service.

Pine Brush Products
Stockingate
Oton Clanford
Staffordshire ST18 9PB
Suppliers of a range of brushes,
milk paints and other artist's
materials.

E. Ploton (Sundries) Ltd
273 Archway Road
London N6 5AA
Suppliers of a wide range of
paints, varnishes and decorating
equipment.

Potmolen Paints
27 Woodstock Industrial
Estate
Warminster
Wiltshire BA12 9DX
Suppliers of conservation-
grade limewashes, casein and
oil-bound distemper, and
biodegradable paint and
varnish strippers.

Putnams Painting &
Designs Ltd
55 Regents Park Road
London NW1 8XD
Suppliers of Mediterranean palette
pigments and paints.

J. H. Ratcliffe & Co (Paints) Ltd
135a Linaker Road
Southport
Lancashire
PR8 5DF
Manufacturers and suppliers of
paints and varnishes.

The Rose of Jericho Ltd
PO Box 53
Kettering
Northhamptonshire
NN14 3BN
Suppliers of a wide range of
traditional paints and materials.

Rustins Ltd
Waterloo Road
London NW2 7TX
Suppliers of a range of paints,
varnishes and restoration products.

Simpsons Paints Ltd
122–4 Broadley Street
London NW8 8BB
Suppliers of specialist brushes
and artist's materials.

Stuart R. Stevenson
68 Clerkenwell Road
London EC1M 5QA
Suppliers of artist's materials.

Wood Finishes
30 The Vineyard
Richmond
Surrey TW10 6AN
Suppliers of lacquer paint, powder
pigments and spirit dyes.

UNITED STATES

Paints and materials

Absolute Coatings, Inc
34 Industrial Street
Bronx NY 10461
Suppliers of varnishes.

Adele Bishop
PO Box 3349
CL40
Kinston NC 28501
Suppliers of stencils (traditional
and modern designs), paints and
brushes. Also mail order.

Antique Color Supply Inc
PO Box 711
Harvard
Massachusetts MA 01451
Suppliers of traditional milk paints
in a wide range of colors.

Art Supply Warehouse
360 Main Avenue (Route 7)
Norwalk CT 06851
Retail suppliers of artists' paints,
brushes and general art supplies.
Offers a mail order service.

Dick Blick Fine Art Company
PO Box 1276
Galesburg IL 61401
Artists' paints, brushes and general
art supplies.

Brosse et Dupont
3 Milltown Court
Union NJ 07083
Importers of a wide range of
standard and specialist brushes.

Central Art
1126 Walnut Street
Philadelphia PA 19017
Artists' paints, brushes and general
supplies.

Albert Constantine & Son Inc
2050 Eastchester Road
Bronx NY 10461
Suppliers of paint strippers,
brushes and varnishes.

Country Accents
PO Box 437
Montoursville
Pennsylvania PA 17754
Suppliers of punched
tin panels.

Dover Publications
11 East Ninth Avenue
New York NY 10019
Suppliers of reference books,
period paints and stencils
by catalogue and mail
order.

Favor-Ruhl
23 S. Wabash
Chicago
Illinois IL 60603
Suppliers of a wide range
of paints.

Flax's
1699 Market Street
San Francisco
California CA 94103
Suppliers of a wide range
of paints.

Sam Flax, Inc
39 West 19th Street
New York NY 10011
General art and graphic art
supplies.

Floorcloths by Ingrid
8 Randall Road
Rochester
Massachusetts MA 02770
Suppliers of traditional
stencilled and hand-painted
floorcloths.

Good and Company
Floorclothmakers at
Salzburg Square
Route 101
Amherst
New Hampshire 03031
*Suppliers of traditional stencilled
and hand-painted floorcloths.*

Frog Tool Company Ltd
700 West Jackson Boulevard
Chicago IL 60606
*Suppliers of paint strippers,
brushes and varnishes.*

Fuller-O'Brien Corp
450 East Grand Avenue
South San Francisco CA 84080
*Suppliers of a wide range of
decorating materials and
equipment.*

Gail Grisi Stencilling, Inc
PO Box 1263
Haddonfield
New Jersey NJ 08033
*Suppliers of pre-cut stencil
designs (over 250 patterns).
They also have retail stores in
New Jersey, and offer a mail order
service.*

Also at:
405 Haddon Avenue
Haddonfield NJ 08033

**Grand Central Artists'
Materials, Inc**
18 East 40th Street
New York NY 10016
General art and graphic art supplies.

**Janovic Plasa's Incomplete
catalog**
30–35 Thompson Avenue
Long Island City NY 11101
*Catalog of materials and
equipment.*

Koenig Artists' Supply Corp.
1777 Boston Post Road
Milford CT 06460
General art supplies.

Lee's Art Shop, Inc
220 West 57th Street
New York NY 10019
*General art supplies, including
color mixing charts.*

Lefranc & Bourgeois, Inc
357 Cottage Street
PO Box 2484
Springfield MA 01101 2484
*Distributors of artists' paints
and brushes.*

Liberty Prints
Routes 66 and 23B
Hudson NY 12534
*Suppliers of a wide range of paints,
glazes and brushes.*

Long Island Paint Company
1 Continental Hill
Glen Cove NY 11542
*Suppliers of paints, including
casein-based.*

McCloskey Varnish Company
7600 State Road
Philadelphia PA 19136
*Suppliers of ready-mixed glazes,
flatting oil and varnishes.*

Mohawk Finishing Products Inc
Route 30 North
Amsterdam NY 12010

Also at:
1355 Chattahoochee Avenue NW
PO Box 20074
Howell Mill Station
Atlanta GA 75236
Also at:
4653 Mint Way
Dallas TX 75236

Also at:
1946 East Devon Avenue
Elk Grove Village IL 60007
Also at:
15622 Producer Lane
Huntingdon Beach CA 92649
Suppliers of polishes and shellacs.

**National Trust for Historical
Preservation**
1785 Massachusetts Ave, NW
Washington DC 20036
*Provides advice and information
on restoration of period houses.*

New York Central Art Supply
62 Third Avenue
New York NY10003
*General art supplies, including
spalters and brushes.*

**The Old Fashioned Milk Paint
Company**
Box 222
Groton MA 01450
Suppliers of milk paints.

Pearl Paint
308 Canal Street
New York NY 10013
*Suppliers of specialist brushes,
art supplies and paints.*

Philadelphia Floorcloths
510 Merwyn Road
Narbert, Pennsylvania PA 19072
Suppliers of traditional floorcloths.

Pottery Barn
100 North Point Street
San Francisco CA 94133
Suppliers of amateur marbling kits.

Pratt & Lambert, Inc
PO Box 22
Buffalo NY 14240
*Suppliers of paints, ready-mixed
glazes and varnishes.*

Renovator's Supply, Inc
Renovator's Old Mill
Millers Falls MA 10349
*General supplies for renovation
and restoration.*

Sappnos Paint
801 West Diversey
Chicago IL 60614
*Suppliers of specialist brushes and
paints.*

Martin Senour Company
1370 Ontario Avenue N.W.
Cleveland
Ohio 44113
Also at:
West Chester Wallpaper
and Paint Co
104 W. Market Street
West Chester
Pennsylvania PA 19380
*Suppliers of authentic period
Williamsburg paint colors.*

**Stencil House of New
Hampshire**
PO Box 109
Hooksett
New Hampshire 03106
*Stencils, acrylic paints, brushes,
brush cleaners etc; by mail
order only.*

Stencil World
1456 Second Avenue
Box 175B
New York NY 10021
*Suppliers of stencils and
stenciling equipment; by mail
order only.*

The Stulb Company
PO Box 597
Allenstown
Pennsylvania PA 18105
*Manufacturers of Williamsburg
buttermilk paint colors.*

Texas Art Supply
2001 Montrose
Houston
Texas 7706
Paint suppliers.

Leo Uhlfelder Company
420 South Fulton Avenue
Mount Vernon NY 10553
*Importers and manufacturers
of decorator's and artist's
brushes.*

Utrecht Manufacturing Corp
33-35th Street
Brooklyn NY 11232
General art supplies.

Winsor & Newton, Inc
11 Constitution Avenue
Piscataway NJ 08855
*Suppliers of artists' paints and
brushes.*

S. Wolf and Sons
771 Ninth Avenue
New York NY 10019
*Suppliers of paints and specialist
brushes.*

**Wood Finishing Supply
Company, Inc**
100 Throop Street
Palmyra NY 14522
*Glazes, steel combs, brushes and
varnishes etc, by mail order.*

Woodcrafter's Lumber Sales, Inc
212 Northeast Sixth Avenue
Portland OR 97232
*Suppliers of paint strippers,
varnishes and brushes.*

Woodcrafter's Supply Corp
5331 Sinclair Road
Columbus OH 43229
*Suppliers of paint strippers and
varnishes.*

Woodworker's Store
21801 Industrial Boulevard
Rogers MN 55374
*Suppliers of paint strippers,
brushes, varnishes and wood fillers.*

Places to visit

BRITAIN

American Museum in Britain
Claverton Manor
Bath
Avon BA2 7BT
*Colonial and Shaker interiors,
furniture and artefacts.*

Charleston Farmhouse
Near Firle
Lewes
East Sussex
BN8 6LL
*Now a museum; this was home to
the "Bloomsbury set" during the
First World War. Contains exam-
ples of hand-painted furniture and
architectural fixtures and fittings.*

Highland Folk Museum
Duke Street
Kingussie PH21 1JG
Scotland
Early local furniture and artefacts.

**Museum of Lakeland Life &
Industry**
Abbot Hall
Kendal
Cumbria LA9 6BT
*Trade workshops and period
interiors, furniture and artefacts,
tools etc.*

Norfolk Rural Life Museum
Grassenhall
East Dereham
Norfolk NR20 4DR
Labourers' cottage and artefacts.

St Fagan's Folk Art Museum
St Fagins
Cardiff CF5 6XB
Wales
*Furnished period cottages, rural
artefacts, tools.*

UNITED STATES

Adirondack Museum
Blue Mountain Lake
New York NY 12812
*Museum depicting the history and
art of the Adirondack region.*

Atlanta Historic Society
3101 Andrews Drive N.W.
Atlanta
Georgia 30305
*Two historic houses: Tullie
Smith House, an 1840s
plantation farm house, and
the Swan House, an Anglo-
Palladian mansion built in
1928. Plus gardens, woodlands
and museum exhibits.*

Colonial Williamsburg
PO Box C
Williamsburg VA 23187
*Early Colonial interiors, furniture
and artefacts.*

Dekalb Historic Society
Old Courthouse
Decatur, Atlanta
Georgia 30030
*The Mary Gay House, Swanton
House, log cabins and rustic barns,
all historically furnished.*

Hancock Shaker Village
Albany Road, Route 20
PO Box 898
Pittsfield MA 02102
*Shaker interiors, furniture,
artefacts, etc.*

Metropolitan Museum of Art
Fifth Avenue at 82nd Street
NY 10028
Rare early furniture and artefacts.

Old Sturbridge Village
1 Old Sturbridge Village Road
Sturbridge
MA 015662
*Colonial-period furniture and
artefacts.*

NORWAY

Glomdalsmuseet
Elverum
Norway
*Restored 17th- and 18th-century
Norwegian houses.*

Of special note:

Mark Done
3 Mountfort Terrace
Barnsbury Square
London N1 1JJ
England
*Specialist decorator who
offers a wide range of
finishes, including marbling,
woodgraining, folk-painting
and faux limewash. He
demonstrated all the decorating
projects shown in this book.*

Stephen Mack
Stephen Mack Associates
Chase Hill Farm, Ashaway
Rhode Island 02804
USA
*Specializes in the reconstruction
and restoration of 17th- and 18th-
century buildings.*

Index

Acknowledgments

THE AUTHOR would like to thank the following in Editorial and
Design for all their hard work during the production of this book:
Judith More, Janis Utton, Julia North, Emma Boys and
Tony Spalding.

THE AUTHOR would also like to offer special thanks to the following
for their invaluable advice and assistance: Käre Svein, Mark Done,
Stephen Mack, Gloria and Eric Stewart, Tasha Miller and
Emily Jewsbury.

THE AUTHOR AND PUBLISHER would also like to thank
Lawrence T. Bridgeman for supplying the milk paints and oil-based
"Old Village" paints used in many of the projects demonstrated in
the book. Thanks also to After Noah, Habitat and Summerville
and Bishop for supplying various props.

THE AUTHOR AND PUBLISHER would like to thank the following
homeowners, interior designers, antique dealers and museums
for allowing special photography:

The Adirondack Museum

The American Museum

The Atlanta Historic Society

Mike Chalon

Charleston Farmhouse

Lisa and Jim Cherry

Christophe Gollut

The Comoglio Showroom

Christophe Decarpentrie

The Durfe House

Jessie Famous

Thomas Young Fearnley

The Glomdalsmuseet

Tony Heaton

Hinchcliffe & Barber

Jack Hill

The Holmenkollen Park
Hotel Rica

Jocasta Innes

Howard Kaplan

Maria Luisa Larranaga,
   Condesa Vde de Foixa

Stephen Mack, of Stephen
Mack Associates

Cindy Makens

Trevor Micklem

Guimond Mounter

Lars Olsson

Jancis Page

Jamie and Janetta Parlade

Jack and Tasha Polizzi

Buddy & Laura Rau

Jacki Sadoun

Sylvie and Peter Schofield

Seaside

Guiseppe and Sarah Sesti

The Shaker Museum

Lars and Ursula Sjoberg

The Skansen Open Air
   Museum

Sally Spillane and
   Robinson Leech

Gloria and Eric Stewart

Michael Wakelin and
   Helen Linfield

Mary Anne Wilkins

Mary Wondrausch